Managing Diversity in Health Care Manual

Managing Diversity in Health Care Manual

PROVEN TOOLS AND ACTIVITIES
FOR LEADERS AND TRAINERS

Lee Gardenswartz • Anita Rowe

Jossey-Bass Publishers
San Francisco

Jossey-Bass books and products are available through most bookstores. To contact Jossey-Bass directly, call (888) 378-2537, fax to (800) 605-2665, or visit our website at www.josseybass.com.

Substantial discounts on bulk quantities of Jossey-Bass books are available to corporations, professional associations, and other organizations. For details and discount information, contact the special sales department at Jossey-Bass.

 Manufactured in the United States of America on Lyons Falls Turin Book. This paper is acid-free and 100 percent totally chlorine-free.

Library of Congress Cataloging-in-Publication Data

Gardenswartz, Lee.
    Managing diversity in health care manual : proven tools and
activities for leaders and trainers / Lee Gardenswartz and Anita
Rowe.
      p. cm.
    Includes bibliographical references (p.)
    ISBN 0-7879-4393-2 (alk. paper)
    1. Transcultural medical care—United States. 2. Diversity in the
workplace—United States. 3. Minorities—medical care—United
States. 4. Minorities—health and hygiene—United States. I. Rowe,
Anita. II. Title.
RA418.5.T73 G37   1999
362.1'068—dc21   99-6145

PB Printing   10 9 8 7 6 5 4 3 2 1

Contents

The Authors

LEE GARDENSWARTZ AND ANITA ROWE began helping organizations with diversity in 1977 while working with the Los Angeles Unified School District to deal with its diversity challenges at the time of mandatory integration. Since that time they have specialized in the "human side of management," working with a variety of regional and national clients—including GTE, Southern California Gas Company, the IRS, the Society of Consumer Affairs Professionals, DWP, *The Los Angeles Times*, FHP, the State of California Department of Health Services, British Telecommunications, UCLA, South Coast AQMD, First State Bank, VA Medical Center, MCA, and The Prudential—helping them to manage change, handle stress, build productive and cohesive work teams, and create intercultural understanding and harmony in the workplace. In addition, they have helped organizations through their writing on diversity.

Their book *Managing Diversity: A Complete Desk Reference and Planning Guide* (1993), which won the book-of-the-year award from the Society for Human Resource Managers in 1994, has served as a primary guide to organizations in structuring their diversity initiatives, providing not only conceptual information but also techniques and tools. They write a regular column in the *Managing Diversity* newsletter; have written articles on diversity for publications such as *Physician Executive, College and University Personnel Journal,* and *Working World;* and have been featured in *Personnel Journal.* They have also coauthored the *Managing Diversity Survival Guide* (1994), *The Diversity Tool Kit* (1994), and *Diverse Teams at Work* (1995).

Gardenswartz and Rowe have lectured widely, giving keynote speeches, facilitating team-building retreats, and teaching seminars across the country. They have made guest appearances on such programs as

Mid-Morning LA, CNN's News Night, Sun Up San Diego, AM Northwest, Crier and Company, and the *Michael Jackson Show.* They also teach about diversity through institutions such as the National Multicultural Institute in Washington, D.C., and the Intercultural Communication Institute in Portland, Oregon.

Lee Gardenswartz is a native of Denver and a graduate of the University of Colorado at Boulder. Anita Rowe is a native of Los Angeles and a graduate of the University of California Los Angeles. Each worked as a secondary teacher and staff development facilitator in the Los Angeles Unified School District for a number of years before returning to academia to earn a Doctorate of Human Behavior from the United States International University in 1981.

Introduction

THIS MANUAL, to be used in conjunction with *Managing Diversity in Health Care*, provides a variety of learning and assessment activities that are relevant, applicable, and designed to help health care professionals grapple with issues of diversity in both the workforce and patient population. The activities stimulate awareness, build knowledge, develop skills, and generate assessment data. This resource is intended for individuals charged with training and educating staff, implementing diversity initiatives, leading discussions of issues faced in serving a wider patient population, and building a more adaptable organization. Even veteran trainers who may have experience conducting training on other topics will find the information and tools they need to conduct effective diversity training. Throughout this manual, the label "trainer" is used to indicate the individual conducting training, although that role requires a combination of both facilitation and training skills. Those required to facilitate diversity sessions will find the activities and processes in this resource as applicable as trainers will.

Part One offers information to prepare the trainer for the experience of conducting diversity sessions. A trainer competency self-assessment is provided, as well as guidelines for designing agendas, assessing needs, and evaluating the effectiveness of training interventions.

Part Two provides a series of training activities that are grouped by content areas that correspond to the content areas in *Managing Diversity in Health Care*. Lecturette information to support the learning activities is found in each of the chapters. Each activity is carefully structured to accomplish specific objectives. In fact, many of the learning activities are designed to accomplish similar objectives. As a result, the trainer has many options from which to select appropriate learning activities for any audience, educational level, and purpose, as well as to suit his or her own preferences for different learning modes. The matrix of activities found on pages 3 and 4 following this introduction provides a cross reference for the tools to help in selecting the most relevant learning activities for particular audiences.

Part Three provides an annotated list of resources for additional information about the issues and topics that emerge when discussing and learning about diversity. The listing is grouped first by medium, whether book or other resource, then according to content area, such as African-American, Latino, gender, or health care issues.

MANAGING DIVERSITY IN HEALTH CARE ACTIVITY MATRIX

Learning Activities	Audiences								Issues					
	All Employees	Managers	Patient Service Staff	Trainers	Human Resources Staff	Executives	Volunteers	Stereotypes	Cultural Differences	Communication	Team Building	Leadership	Systems Changes	Needs Assessment
Chapter 4: Why Diversity Is Good for Business														
Changing Demographics: Do You Know Your Patients?	X	X	X	X	X	X	X							X
Changing Demographics: Do You Know Your Workforce?	X	X	X	X	X	X	X							X
Effects of Increased Diversity in the Workforce	X	X	X	X	X	X	X					X	X	X
Effects of Increased Diversity in the Patient Base	X	X	X	X	X	X	X					X	X	X
Chapter 5: The Dimensions of Health Care Diversity														
Four Layers of Diversity	X	X	X	X	X	X	X	X				X	X	
Assessing the Impact of Diversity in Your Health Care Organization	X	X	X	X	X	X	X	X				X	X	X
Analyzing the Influence of Your Own Diversity on You as a Health Care Professional	X	X	X	X	X		X				X			
Assumptions About Appearance	X	X	X	X	X		X	X						
Checking Your Own Comfort with Differences	X	X	X	X	X		X	X		X	X			
Chapter 6: The Truth About Cultural Programming														
Analyzing Your Own Cultural "Software"	X	X	X	X	X	X	X		X		X			
Aspects of Culture: Their Impact in a Health Care Setting	X	X	X	X	X		X		X	X			X	X
Expanding Cultural Interpretations	X	X	X	X	X		X	X	X	X				
Chapter 7: Achieving Practical Cultural Literacy														
Who's Involved in Making Health Care Decisions?		X	X	X					X	X				
How Culturally Sensitive Are You? A Checklist for Care Givers		X	X	X			X		X	X				
Key Cultural Values Impacting Care: My Comfort Zone	X	X	X	X	X	X	X		X		X			
An Overall Glance at Key Cultural Values and How They Impact Care		X	X	X			X		X					

	Audiences							Issues						
Chapter 8: Improving Communication in Diverse Environments	All Employees	Managers	Patient Service Staff	Trainers	Human Resources Staff	Executives	Volunteers	Stereotypes	Cultural Differences	Communication	Team Building	Leadership	Systems Changes	Needs Assessment
Language and You	X	X	X	X	X		X		X	X				
Intercultural Hooks That Block Communication	X	X	X	X	X		X	X	X	X				
Cultural Differences Affecting Communication with Patients and Staff	X	X	X	X	X	X	X			X	X			
Giving Directions and Explanations in Culturally Sensitive Ways	X	X	X	X	X		X			X				
Communicating Across Language Barriers	X	X	X	X	X		X			X			X	
Guidelines for Using Interpreters	X	X	X	X	X	X	X			X			X	
Practice in Conducting Culturally Sensitive Medical Interviews: Using the LEARN Steps		X	X	X					X	X				
Chapter 9: Removing Stereotypes That Block High-Quality Care														
Assumptions: What You See is What You Get	X	X	X	X	X		X	X						
Recognizing Stereotypes	X	X	X	X	X		X	X						
Subjective Factors Influencing Care	X	X	X	X	X		X	X						
Comments and Behaviors That May Indicate Stereotypes and Prejudice	X	X	X	X	X	X	X	X						X
From a Different Perspective	X	X	X	X	X	X	X	X	X					
Systemic Points of Contact: Where Stereotypes Can Have an Impact		X		X	X	X		X			X	X	X	
You As the Object of Stereotypes	X	X	X	X	X		X	X			X			
Chapter 10: The Diversity Leadership Challenge														
Diversity Accountability Questionnaire		X		X	X	X						X	X	X
Creating a Climate That Results in Top Performance and High Morale	X	X		X	X	X					X	X	X	
Climate Survey	X	X		X	X	X					X	X	X	X
Leadership Characteristics Questionnaire		X		X	X	X						X	X	X
Leadership Characteristics Questionnaire Assessment		X		X	X	X						X	X	
Diversity: Staff Expectation Survey	X	X		X	X	X						X	X	X
Chapter 11: Overcoming Barriers to Change														
Testing Commitment from the Top		X		X	X	X						X	X	X
Serving Diverse Patients and Families: An Assessment Questionnaire	X	X	X	X	X	X	X		X	X		X	X	X
Managing Diversity Questionnaire	X	X	X	X	X	X	X					X	X	X
Problem-Solving Response Sheet	X	X	X	X	X	X	X				X	X	X	
Behaviors of an Effective Health Care Employee in a Pluralistic Environment	X	X	X	X	X	X	X				X	X		

Part One

Preparation for Success

PART ONE OFFERS INFORMATION to prepare the trainer for the experience of conducting diversity sessions. A trainer competency self-assessment is provided, as well as guidelines for designing training sessions, structuring the agenda, assessing needs, and evaluating the effectiveness of training interventions.

Chapter 1

Orienting Yourself to Diversity Training

BEFORE DESIGNING AND CONDUCTING DIVERSITY TRAINING, it is essential to understand some of the realities you will face when you step into this arena. To prepare yourself for this role, Chapter 1 helps you by discussing the challenges you may face, providing guidelines for dealing with them, and giving you an opportunity to assess your own competencies as a diversity trainer.

Challenges of Diversity Training

Welcome to diversity training, an ongoing developmental process that is not "business as usual." Helping people come to terms with differences and deal with diversity is more complex than many other types of training. It presents some significant challenges because it requires more of trainers and more of participants. Among these challenges are the following:

Heightened Emotions and Tension

Diversity is a high affect topic. There are very few right and wrong answers, and there are many sensitive issues about which there are apt to be strong feelings and vehement opinions. In a society that tells us it is wrong to be prejudiced, just talking about these topics breaks social taboos—and hence produces tension. Most of us find it difficult to face and admit our own biases and stereotypical assumptions. In addition, the changes brought about by increasing diversity are sometimes frustrating and difficult to deal with. As a result, anger, confusion, upset, and dismay are not uncommon. Building an accepting, safe training environment in which people feel comfortable voicing these feelings is essential.

Danger of Polarization

An age-old dictum warns us not to talk about religion or politics at parties for fear that a polarizing argument will ensue. That same dictum could be reframed around issues of race, ethnicity, sexual orientation, and many other dimensions. In diversity training sessions, there is a danger of participants falling into an either/or trap when discussing topics that bring out strong emotional reactions and entrenched opinions, such as those regarding language ("Should we have English-only rules?") or gay and lesbian rights ("Should gays be allowed in the military?"). These polarizing discussions create arguments and no-win situations that can split a group into warring camps.

One role of training is to help the group see other options and develop ways of looking at each situation in a new light. It is also helpful to steer the discussion to situations, practices, and policies participants have some control over and away from opinions and arguments about values that are dead ends. Exercises and discussion questions that help participants see both sides of an issue and a variety of possible solutions are included in the directions for many of the activities in Part Two.

People with Personal Axes to Grind

Trainees bring their own baggage into diversity sessions and, in some cases, a backlog of unresolved issues can disrupt the learning of others. Some may even see a diversity training session as the place to air gripes and take care of problems. Focusing on examples, such as one poorly handled organizational problem or one particular incident of discrimination, can skew the discussion, polarize the group, and take the training away from its main points. Clear objectives, a well-structured agenda, and strong facilitation skills are required to keep such a group on track.

People Being Boxed into Corners

Because of the strongly held opinions about many diversity issues, it is easy for individuals to box one another into corners with personal attacks and labels. This can lead to resentful withdrawal ("Well, I guess I'd better not say anything, because everything I say is considered prejudiced,") or judgmental attacks ("Wow, what a racist comment!"). It is important to create a climate in which everyone is treated with respect and in which no one loses dignity. For the trainer, this means establishing and adhering to ground rules and making observations that suggest a different response, such as, "Racist is a label. I've heard it said that we're all recovering racists and sexists and that we can all continue to learn and grow."

A Wide Range of Reactions

In diversity sessions, a wide variety of reactions and attitudes, from denial and hostility to acceptance and relief that the training is finally taking place, are common. Some trainees will make claims denying that there are any problems, saying things such as, "We all get along here" or "I'm not prejudiced. I treat everyone the same." Others may be angry about having to attend the sessions: "Why are we spending money on this when I just took a 5 percent pay cut?" Some may be upset about the changing demographics: "When in Rome, do as the Romans do. Why do I have to learn about them?" Finally, others may be delighted and welcome the training: "It's about time we talked about these issues." Creating a climate in which these different views can be both expressed and addressed needs to be part of the agenda.

Facilitating discussions that encourage an airing of views without producing arguments is a challenge that requires the trainer's full attention and quick responses. It helps to acknowledge the range of views and state that one of the reasons you are meeting in the first place is because of that broad range of views. It is also beneficial to let people know at the beginning that sharing different perceptions is one of the objectives, whereas coming to consensus is not an objective.

The expectation that participants will learn something new or see something differently as a result of their experiences in the session can be suggested by challenging participants in a particular activity to be surprised or hear a different perspective and by reminding participants that there are no right or wrong responses when discussing perceptions, values, and opinions.

White Male Bashing

Because white males have been the dominant group in American society and business, it is tempting to make them the target of blame. It is important to help trainees see that all of us are products of socialization and cultural programming and that no one group has the corner on the market when it comes to discrimination and prejudice. Activities that help participants look beyond labels and assumptions and see the complexity of each human being are essential. For example, information and activities in Chapter 5 in this book and Chapter 2 in *Managing Diversity in Health Care*, which explore the many dimensions of diversity, and in Chapter 9 in this book and Chapter 6 in *Managing Diversity in Health Care*, which deal with stereotypes, are relevant. It is also useful to allow an airing of the difficulties and dilemmas white males face as they adapt in today's increasingly diverse and rapidly changing workplace.

A Perception That Training Is for the Benefit of Others

Resistance sometimes arises in diversity training sessions when people view diversity as relevant for others rather than for themselves. Resentment ("Why do we have to do all this for them?") and detachment from the issue ("What does diversity have to do with me?") are common responses. As a result, it is important to emphasize both the benefit of the training for everyone and an inclusive definition that takes everyone's situation into account. Chapters 1 and 2 in *Managing Diversity in Health Care* provide a great deal of information that addresses these points. You can help participants understand these concepts by explaining how the training session can help them deal with some of the challenges diversity brings. The activities in Chapter 5 of the book, which explore the many dimensions of diversity and show that everyone is a part of the diversity equation, and those from Chapter 4, which lead participants to analyze the benefits as well as the challenges of diversity, help make this point.

Danger of Giving Lip Service

Diversity training often raises expectations, causing employees to have hope for more equitable treatment and increased opportunity. Doing diversity training because it is the latest fad in the business magazines or because someone in Human Resources thinks it is important is a setup for disappointment. Training needs to be a part of a larger plan that ties into your organization's strategic objectives. Having the real support of senior management means you will be able to remove systems obstacles and make policy changes that are necessary to create a more inclusive organization. If genuine commitment does not accompany the training, participants are apt to discount its value, no matter how well it is done or how useful it is.

Specific suggestions for how to deal with these realities are given in the following segments of this chapter. Guidelines for structuring agendas that deal effectively with them are presented in succeeding chapters of Part One.

Guidelines for Maximizing the Effectiveness of Your Training

Although there are no fail-safe ways to conduct diversity training, the following seven suggestions provide some guidelines as you prepare to structure and lead impactful, productive training sessions.

Create Ground Rules for Your Training

To create a safe environment, it is important to have a framework of acceptable behavior that all participants know, understand, and adhere to. These ground rules should be presented at the beginning, following the objectives, then enforced throughout the session. Keep them short, simple, and behaviorally focused. We have seen many trainers present ground rules in their workshops. We have also seen groups create their own rules, with the help of the trainer, at the beginning of a session. In either case, here are samples of a few frequently used, appropriate ground rules:

- Presume good will;
- Speak for yourself;
- Be open to new ideas;
- Actively participate in the session;
- Avoid side conversations; and
- Refrain from finger pointing, blaming, or personal attacks.

It may also be necessary to take a participant aside if he or she has a specific personal issue to deal with and suggest other avenues for addressing those concerns (for example, Equal Employee Opportunity, Employee Relations, or EAP).

Expect Resistance and Be Prepared to Deal with It

Many factors can influence the mind-sets of participants in your training session. There may have been workplace incidents, previous training session blowups, or unpopular organizational changes. These factors may cause participants to be skeptical or resistant. There is no substitute for doing your homework. Knowing the history will help you anticipate participant reactions and prepare for the worst. Expecting resistance will help you through it and make you less defensive. You can prepare yourself to deal with resistance by trying the following:

- Interviewing a sample of participants ahead of time, eliciting the range of attitudes and issues that may be in the group.
- Openly addressing the hidden agendas or underlying issues with your initial comments. This can validate feelings and let participants know you understand.
- Whenever possible, showing participants how what they will learn in the training can help them address their concerns or deal with their frustrations.

- Allaying fears by stating clearly what the session is and is not about. Say, for example, "We will learn how culture impacts our interactions with patients and learn how to increase our effectiveness in communicating with them. It is not to whitewash issues or enforce political correctness."

- Coopting resistors by giving them a job such as recorder.

- Grouping participants in pairs or small groups for discussion so no resistor has a large audience.

- Bringing balance to discussions by having participants brainstorm pros and cons in small groups. For example, groups can list effective and ineffective ways the organization deals with diversity, meets diverse patient needs, or communicates with employees.

Put Diversity Training in a Larger Organizational Context

Diversity training that is treated like an appendage will never fit into organizational life in a meaningful way, and its value and effectiveness will be short-lived. For example, in organizations in which discrimination persists and advancement opportunities for women and people of color are limited, it is important that diversity training not only deal with how assumptions and stereotypes categorize and limit people, but also provides an avenue for focusing on the organization's promotional and career development systems. Training cannot be expected to carry the entire load for making organizational change. You can help to enlarge the focus by the following means:

- Previewing accompanying organizational changes (for example, job postings, pay equity reviews, hiring of full-time interpreters, or increasing the flexibility of benefits).

- Explaining other diversity processes that are in place (for example, the formation of a Diversity Council or an upcoming survey).

- Reviewing the organization's plans and goals (for example, target customer service improvement goals).

- Talking with your administrator, CEO, and/or other top managers to clarify their reasons for embarking on this training process, as well as to see how diversity fits into the overall strategic goals of the institution.

- Gaining an understanding of the organization's diversity strategy, the part training plays in that strategy, and any aspects of the plan that deal with systems and policy changes.

Help Participants Understand the Role of Socialization

Diversity training is challenging and demanding work. It involves not only teaching new skills, but also looking at values, belief systems, and fundamental paradigms about how the world works and who is entitled to what. No other type of training puts the individual and all that he or she is under the microscope so closely. In no other training sessions are participants' values and belief systems, absorbed osmosis-like from infancy, under such tight scrutiny. It is often both startling and upsetting for people to have to dust off racist phrases learned from their parents or to acknowledge early incidents of discrimination. The role socialization plays stuns participants once they become aware of it. For example, participants in one session we conducted were twins, one male and one female. They shared with the group that the young man had been programmed by his parents to go to college and earn advanced degrees. His very bright sister was slotted, without her input, for marriage and parenting immediately after high school. That experience gave attendees pause. It caused everyone to examine the personal programming they had experienced about their own capabilities, as well as the messages they had received about the expectations of other racial, gender, ethnic, or cultural groups. Many of the activities in Chapters 5 and 6 in this workbook address this point.

Understand the Complexity of the Issues

Diversity-related issues are complex because so many norms, traditions, rituals, and values come under scrutiny. The study of cultures and subcultures may be fascinating, but it is not easy because human nature tends to make us all ethnocentric, seeing the world from the perspectives of our own backgrounds and using them as the standard. Positive experiences and exposure to diverse people and groups can make us more tolerant of behavior different from our own. Just by looking at subcultures in the United States based on geography, race, and ethnicity, we can see that no one way is better than another; rather, all norms have both positive and negative value. The challenge is helping employees come to terms with the many variations that co-workers bring to the organization or work team. Amidst all this variety, it is important to create a common organizational culture with goals, values, and expectations strong enough to hold the group together. Activities that help people focus on common ground and shared values are helpful here. Those in Chapters 6 and 7 focus on this aspect.

Accept That the End Result of Diversity Is a *Fundamental Redistribution of Resources and Power*

Every change brings losses and gains. Coming to terms with this reality is not easy because most people focus on what they will lose. For those who have been part of the dominant group, diversity changes often mean loss. As a diversity trainer, it is critical that you frame your concepts and discussion in a way that does not pit people and groups against one another and that does enable participants to see what they stand to gain with changes and what they may lose by keeping the status quo. Activities in Chapter 4 in this workbook focus on this point.

Make Sure the Person Who Champions Your Program Has Credibility and Clout

If the responsibility for implementation or advocacy of the diversity program belongs to someone without positional and/or personal power in the organization, this will decrease the significance of the training in the eyes of the participants. If you cannot obtain top-level support, and if your assignment does not come from someone who has respect and influence throughout the organization, the message will be obvious to all employees. Over the years, the savvy troops have learned what the CEO's pet projects are by who advocates and implements them. Similarly, they will know where diversity training ranks in importance when they learn who beats the drums for such a program. Asking the CEO, administrator, or other senior manager to participate actively in training and to introduce sessions, explaining why diversity training is important to the organization's success, can help make the program a success.

Responses to Diversity-Related Comments, Concerns, and Emotions

Some of the most frequently asked questions at diversity train-the-trainer sessions and by managers of diverse groups center around ways to respond to tough, emotionally charged situations. Whether the situation is the result of a prejudicial remark, an angry question, a stereotypical judgment, or a frustrated outburst, it's often a show-stopper. The following are typical of emotionally laden comments that emerge during diversity training:

- "I don't care what anyone is, but why do they have to tell us?"
- "How am I supposed to know the correct terminology today? Is it black or African-American? Lady or female? Latino, Hispanic, or Chicano?"

- "Everyone's so sensitive; you can't have fun anymore."
- "My grandparents learned English. Why can't they?"
- "Why do I have to learn about them? They're in this country now!"

Responding to these questions and statements can be difficult. Yet each gives you an opportunity to set the tone, teach about diversity, and demonstrate your commitment to creating a truly inclusive, respectful work environment. Effective responses are as varied as the questions and the personalities of responders; however, a few suggestions are given below that may help you frame your responses without coming across as the Politically Correct (PC) Police Thought Patrol that tries to squelch dialogue, shut down discussion, and create greater discomfort.

Inquire

Rather than jump to conclusions, ask questions to understand, clarify, or find out more information. Dig deeper to discover what the person means and what reasoning is behind the comment or question. Just make sure your inquiry is a real search for information, not an off-putting accusation. Try some of these probes:

- "What makes you say that?"
- "Is that a problem you've faced?"
- "Can you tell us more about that?"
- "How does this impact your interactions with patients or physicians?"

Show Empathy

When powerful emotions are present, acknowledging and responding to the feelings expressed is an important first step in defusing the situation. This means listening not just to the words, but to the "melody," the underlying feelings. Undoubtedly you have faced frustrations similar to those faced by the individual you are talking with. Responding empathically demonstrates understanding that can help calm the upset individual so that further communication can take place. Here are some samples of the types of empathic responses you can make:

- "It is frustrating when you can't understand someone."
- "It's difficult to help when you don't know if you're being understood."
- "That is irritating for me, too."
- "Dealing with situations like that is stressful."

Educate and Build Awareness

Once the emotional cloud has dissipated, you have a "teachable moment," a chance to debunk myths, give facts, and explain. Here is where your background and knowledge about stereotypes, cultural differences, and civil rights can be beneficial, as in the following examples:

- "Minorities are the majority in six of the eight largest urban areas in the United States."

- "Did you know that the first civil rights law was passed right after the Civil War, over 130 years ago?"

- "The term 'gypped' comes from Gypsy."

- "Many gays and lesbians prefer 'sexual orientation' over 'sexual preference,' as it expresses their sense that one's sexuality is not a choice but how someone is born."

- "Many women dislike being called a 'lady' in a work situation, as it is a social rather than a professional term, much like gentleman."

- "Imagine you went to work in a hospital in Brazil. What language would you speak with co-workers from your own country?"

Express Your Feelings

When your feelings are involved, you have a right to let the other person know the impact of the comment. Use nonblaming "I" statements to give your reactions, such as the following:

- "I feel diminished when I'm referred to as a 'gal'."

- "I get upset with jokes about other religions or cultures."

- "I'm uncomfortable when we make us-versus-them generalizations."

- "It bothers me when someone is left out."

State Your Needs or Expectations

If you desire different behavior from the group, let people know what you do and do not want. Here are some ideas:

- "Jokes about religions or cultural groups are off limits with me."

- "Let's focus on creating an approach we can all agree on."

- "Let's spend time figuring out what we can do about the issue, rather than rehashing what's wrong."

Avoid Polarization

Becoming "stuck" in either/or, devil-versus-deep-blue-sea choices is a deadly trap. You can help people avoid this by soliciting other options and points of view, using remarks like the following:

- "What might be some other reasons for this behavior?"
- "What is another way to respond?"
- "Are these our only two options?"
- "How might someone from a different background see this?"
- "What other strategies might work?"

Silence

Although silence can be interpreted as tacit approval, there are times when "no response" is deafening and sends a powerful message of disapproval. Not laughing at a joke or not responding to a sarcastic quip may serve as the only response needed.

Avoid Argument and Defensiveness

Curb the impulse to debate, persuade, argue, or defend your point of view. Doing so generally only strengthens the resistance and drives entrenched opinions deeper. One of the most difficult diversities of all to deal with may be that of differences in values. Acknowledging that we can have differences of opinion, yet respect one another, also demonstrates your ability to walk the talk of diversity.

Answers to Questions That Can Sabotage Your Efforts

Whether you are selling diversity training to the administration or to the participants in your sessions, you need to answer certain questions, both stated and unstated, up front. If not dealt with, these questions can plant the seeds of resistance and undermine your results. Some of the questions most frequently heard regarding diversity and the answers to them are given in the following paragraphs. Before you embark on training, be sure you can answer these questions easily.

"Why Are We Doing This?" An explanation of demographic changes in the work force and patient base, followed by additional information about the population shifts in your region and in your organization specifically, is a start. You may add a discussion of changes that participants have seen and that are presently being dealt with in both the organization and the patient base and how those changes impact participants daily on the job.

"What Has Diversity Got to Do with Us?" This question may require an explanation of the business imperative that diversity presents, both showing that the organization's long-term survival is at stake as well as pointing out the pragmatic benefits to the participants. For example, learning how to communicate across language barriers may be especially helpful to supervisors of employees who speak limited English or to staff who deal with a multicultural patient base. Developing strategies for resolving conflicts may be useful to managers with dysfunctional teams. Developing cross-cultural medical interviewing skills may give physicians and nurses the tools they need to work more effectively with diverse patients.

"What Is Diversity?" Even in sophisticated organizations, a definition of terms is in order, as initially people may limit diversity discussions to race and gender. It is important to have a common frame of reference and a clear definition to minimize confusion. A short lecturette, followed by a discussion of the four layers and multiple dimensions of diversity, may help attendees understand that we are all part of the diversity puzzle and that diversity goes way beyond race and gender. (See Chapter 2 in *Managing Diversity in Health Care.*) Frequently, this broader definition helps clarify the business imperative for resistant participants. The discussion also gives participants a chance to share how these dimensions affect them and their staffs and what the consequences are in terms of patient care.

"What Is the Difference Between Managing Diversity and Affirmative Action?" Often participants make comments that indicate their confusion about the difference between affirmative action and managing diversity. "Isn't this just affirmative action with a new coat of paint?," they ask. An explanation of the key differences—clarifying the various motivations, strategies, and objectives of these initiatives—may be helpful at this point. Especially useful may be making a distinction among legal, moral, and pragmatic organizational motivations. The chart entitled "Affirmative Action, Valuing Differences and Managing Diversity Compared," in *Managing Diversity: A Complete Desk Reference and Planning Guide* (Gardenswartz and Rowe, 1998), offers a concise explanation.

"Does This Mean We Have to Lower Our Standards?" Perceptions of quality versus diversity are at the root of this question. Resistance may arise among participants who think the emphasis on diversity is antithetical to quality. Those with this opinion think that recruiting a more diverse group of employees will reduce quality and that hiring for diversity will be seen as a higher priority than hiring for competence. Dealing with this question may call for a discussion of different ways to view the relationship between quality and diversity. Of course, the important point is that quality and diversity are not mutually exclusive; they can and do occur in the same staff member, physician, manager, or patient.

You, the trainer, are the most critical tool in training for diversity. It is essential to prepare yourself well. Your ability to facilitate learning, answer questions, and deal with tough situations depends on the confidence you feel about this topic. The questionnaire on the next few pages gives you a chance to assess yourself in five areas of critical knowledge, skill, and competence for diversity training.

DIVERSITY TRAINER SELF-ASSESSMENT QUESTIONNAIRE

Directions: To assess your own competence and effectiveness as a diversity trainer, answer the following questions as honestly and accurately as possible.

	Almost Always	Sometimes	Almost Never
1. My own feelings, attitudes, ideas, and values concerning diversity sneak up on me.			
2. The most productive organizations or work groups are those in which no one feels left out.			
3. I understand how culture shapes human behavior.			
4. I am able to present complex ideas simply and make them understood.			
5. I can accurately read a group's mood or tone.			
6. My own assumptions and stereotypes surprise me.			
7. It is stimulating to work with people who don't share my values.			
8. I can talk knowledgeably about the civil rights and other liberation movements.			
9. My energy keeps groups involved and attentive.			
10. I am comfortable confronting and negotiating with others.			
11. I find it difficult to keep my cool in the face of ideas that are offensive to me.			
12. I value a wide range of views and attitudes.			

Source: Adapted with permission from *The Managing Diversity Survival Guide.* © Lee Gardenswartz and Anita Rowe. Burr Ridge, IL: Irwin Professional, 1994.

	Almost Always	Sometimes	Almost Never
13. I am a keen observer of human nature.			
14. I am comfortable speaking to groups of varying size and background.			
15. I can create a nonthreatening, high trust learning environment.			
16. I'm in tune with my own biases.			
17. It bothers me to see people discounted because of age, gender, race, or any other diversity dimension.			
18. I continuously read and study up on contemporary issues related to the various groups represented in my organization.			
19. I am able to tell relevant anecdotes that hold people's interest.			
20. In high conflict situations, I can facilitate discussion so that all viewpoints are aired.			
21. I'm not carrying a banner for any group or viewpoint.			
22. Diversity works when all sides make adaptations.			
23. Comparing cultural norms, inside the United States and beyond its borders, is interesting to me.			
24. I have effective techniques for dealing with disruptive participants.			
25. I can intervene at the appropriate time without threatening others.			

SCORING THE SELF-ASSESSMENT QUESTIONNAIRE

Score numbers 1, 6, and 11 first, and then record the score next to its corresponding number below.

Almost Never = 4 points   Sometimes = 2 points   Almost Always = 0 points

Then score the remaining twenty-two items by recording the score next to the appropriate number.

Almost Always = 4 points   Sometimes = 2 points   Almost Never = 0 points

Trainer as Tool	Belief in Core Diversity Values	Content Knowledge	Platform Skills	Facilitation Skills
1 _____	2 _____	3 _____	4 _____	5 _____
6 _____	7 _____	8 _____	9 _____	10 _____
11 _____	12 _____	13 _____	14 _____	15 _____
16 _____	17 _____	18 _____	19 _____	20 _____
21 _____	22 _____	23 _____	24 _____	25 _____

INTERPRETING THE SELF-ASSESSMENT QUESTIONNAIRE

Points	
80 to 100	You're on the way to becoming an excellent diversity trainer.
60 to 79	You have some of the pieces in place, but you need to do some work to develop your competence in certain areas.
59 and below	Look at the key concepts measured here. If low scores are in platform and facilitation skills, work in these areas can greatly improve your competence. If knowledge is a low area, you can read up and learn. The resource section, which begins on page 221 of *Managing Diversity in Health Care,* is a good place to begin. If, however, low scores are around core values, rethink your commitment to diversity training. Perhaps that's not the best field of training for you.

The questionnaire measures your ability as a diversity trainer in five areas. An explanation of each is given below.

Trainer as Tool

This concept involves the trainer's awareness about how prejudice, stereotypes, assumptions, and all the "-isms" in general, impact him or her. Effective diversity training requires trainers with no "axes to grind," people who will not work through their own issues in the group, nor be "hooked" by people who hold views that are personally repugnant.

A score under 16 on this dimension may mean that you have work to do around the issue before undertaking an assignment for diversity training. Evaluate individual items with low scores and find ways to work around your tendencies before beginning a training session.

Belief in Core Diversity Values

Diversity training has at its center a set of beliefs. Among them are that "diversity is an inside job." This means that we all need to find the comfort and security inside ourselves to deal with "differentness." Diversity implies inclusion, tolerance, adaptation, and equality. It is essential that any diversity trainer subscribe to these values.

A score under 16 on this dimension may mean that you have work to do around the issue before undertaking an assignment for diversity training. Evaluate individual items with low scores and find ways to work around your tendencies before beginning a training session.

Content Knowledge

The body of knowledge about diversity draws on theories from anthropology, psychology, and sociology. It gives information on human behavior, both in groups and individually. It also is focused on awareness of stereotypes and prejudice, culture as a prime shaper of behavior, and management skills adapted to heterogeneous, pluralistic organizations. A good beginning point for increasing your own content knowledge in this area is *Managing Diversity in Health Care*. Other useful resources are found in the Resources section at the end of that book.

A score under 16 on this dimension may mean that you have work to do around the issue before undertaking an assignment for diversity training. Evaluate individual items with low scores and find ways to work around your tendencies before beginning a training session.

Platform Skills

The abilities to instruct, inspire, hold people's attention, provoke thought and discussion and, in general, create a rich, stimulating, and results-oriented learning session depend in large part on the trainer's platform skills. These skills focus on presence and poise in training situations.

A score under 16 on this dimension may mean that you have work to do around the issue before undertaking an assignment for diversity training. Evaluate individual items with low scores and find ways to work around your tendencies before beginning a training session.

Facilitation Skills

The ability to structure the group's processes and design an involving session around complex issues is a key skill for a trainer. Further, an excellent trainer affords dignity and respect to all participants and keeps the group on task while also being flexible enough to change direction as needed. Trainers, especially in diversity training, have the job of creating a safe, nonthreatening environment in which all ideas are heard.

A score under 16 on this dimension may mean that you have work to do around the issue before undertaking an assignment for diversity training. Evaluate individual items with low scores and find ways to work around your tendencies before beginning a training session.

If you need more information to improve either platform or facilitation skills, one good resource is *The New Fieldbook for Trainers: Tips, Tools and Techniques* by John E. Jones and William L. Bearley (1996).

Directions for Using the Diversity Trainer Self-Assessment Questionnaire

Objectives

- To provide organizations with guidelines for selecting potential diversity trainers;

- To enable diversity trainers to identify critical competencies; and

- To assess one's areas of strength and weakness as a diversity trainer.

Intended Audience

- Diversity trainers, consultants, or human resource (HR) professionals who will be conducting training and/or facilitating diversity discussions and activities;

- Trainers or consultants considering the field of diversity training; and

- Human resource professionals hiring diversity trainers.

Time
- $1\frac{1}{4}$ hours.

Materials
- Copies of the Diversity Trainer Self-Assessment Questionnaire for all participants.

- Pens or pencils.

- An easel and newsprint pad.

- Felt-tipped markers.

- An overhead projector (optional).

Suggested Procedures
- Explain that in some ways diversity training is like any other training, but that in other ways it is more demanding because the topic evokes heightened emotions and feelings about acceptance and rejection, involves discrimination, and requires being comfortable with differences and accepting people for who they are. Explain that looking at the complexity of human nature, individually and collectively, with cultural variables, requires great trainer skill, content knowledge, and personal balance. Tell participants that the questionnaire is designed to help them identify their strengths and weaknesses as they look at five critical competencies.

- Hand out the questionnaire and tell participants to answer questions as honestly as possible.

- When they are finished, have participants score their own questionnaires. If the instrument is used in a training setting, depending on group size and purpose, you may want to record scores anonymously on a flip chart to see the range.

- Explain the five competencies and their relevance for being an effective diversity trainer.

- Have participants discuss the questions you list on the overhead or newsprint in pairs or small groups.

- Lead a total group discussion of the questions below.

- Ask participants to respond to the following open-ended statements as a closing activity:

  "My greatest strength as a diversity trainer is. . . ."

  "What I most need to focus on to improve my training is. . . ."

Questions for Discussion

- What is your reaction to the five competencies? What questions do you have about any of them?

- Which of the five areas is your strong suit? Which is your weakest?

- When you look at your low scores, do you see any cluster or pattern?

- Which of your low-score items, if not addressed, has the most potential for damaging your credibility and effectiveness?

- What suggestions do you have for improvement? [Brainstorm ideas from the whole group, then tell participants to use those that seem relevant and helpful as part of their own improvement plans.]

- What specific actions can you take to improve in your low-score areas, based on the data you see here?

Caveats and Considerations

- Before presenting this questionnaire to the group, take it yourself.

Chapter 2
Designing Training Sessions

STRUCTURING YOUR TRAINING AGENDAS requires careful planning. You must take into consideration participant needs as well as design principles for adult learning. This chapter provides guidance for designing and planning diversity training sessions that generate learner involvement, meet the needs of your organization, and achieve the desired learning objectives.

Assessment of Needs

A first step in designing training is identifying the specific diversity obstacles and issues faced by the organization, as well as the needs and concerns of participants. Armed with this information, you can build agendas that address real needs and generate commitment from employees to applying their learning on the job.

Needs can be assessed in a variety of ways. Structured interviews and informal one-on-one conversations with a cross-section of employees will give you much information about conditions, concerns, and frustrations. Less time-consuming than interviewing is the use of focus groups for data gathering. Groups of employees (the focus group) can be brought together for the specific purpose of sharing their perceptions of issues and concerns. Staff members can be grouped according to dimension (such as age, ethnicity, job classification, department) or the group can be mixed. Discussion can be led by a designated facilitator, who is guided by a series of questions. A third method of assessing needs is through the use of a paper and pencil questionnaire or checklist. The list of Symptoms Indicating a Need for Diversity Training that follows is an example of such a checklist. An in-depth comparison of these methodologies, as well as additional information about assessing needs and conducting audits through interviews, focus groups, and questionnaires, can be found in Chapter 11 of *Managing Diversity* (Gardenswartz & Rowe, 1998).

Directions for Using the Symptoms Indicating a Need for Diversity Training Checklist

Objectives

- To investigate the need for training.

- To clarify issues that need to be addressed in training.

Intended Audience

- Trainers responsible for delivering diversity training.

- Employees at all levels.

Time

- 20 to 30 minutes.

Training Materials

- Copies of Symptoms Indicating a Need for Diversity Training checklist for all participants.

- Pens and pencils.

- An easel with newsprint pad (optional).

- Felt-tipped markers (optional).

Suggested Procedures

- Give participants copies of the questionnaire and ask them to check those symptoms they have observed in their organizations.

- If you are using the questionnaire for needs assessment, collect the checklists and tally the results for use in planning.

- Present the data to participants in the resulting training, building a case for the objectives of the session.

- If you are using it for a focus group needs assessment, lead a group discussion of those items checked, charting information about each symptom that is discussed.

Discussion Questions

- Which symptoms did you check?

- How frequently does each occur?

- What is the consequence of each behavior or condition that you checked?

- What knowledge or skills might help you and others deal with the issues underlying these symptoms?

- How might the perception of some of these symptoms change, depending on the departmental area or level?

Caveats and Considerations

- You or the participants can add to the list of symptoms or can brainstorm your own lists.

💾 SYMPTOMS INDICATING A NEED FOR DIVERSITY TRAINING

Directions: Check any symptoms you have observed in your organization.

☐ Complaints about insensitive comments being made or jokes being told in the work unit about age, gender, race, ethnicity, sexual orientation, or physical ability.

☐ Difficulty in retaining employees, particularly those of nondominant groups.

☐ Open conflict between people of different races, ethnicities, and backgrounds or native language groups, ages, and so forth.

☐ Lack of diversity throughout all levels of the organization.

☐ Cultural faux pas.

☐ Complaints about languages other than English being spoken in the workplace.

☐ Complaints about language-related blocks in communication.

☐ Misinterpretation or failure to understand directions that results in mistakes, the repeating of tasks, and low productivity.

☐ Equal Employment Opportunity (EEO) suits and grievances.

☐ Employees feeling isolated and unconnected to their work groups.

☐ Employees perceiving that their strengths and backgrounds are not valued for the unique contribution they can make.

☐ Complaints and judgments about the behavior of certain groups of patients and their families.

☐ Frequent "us versus them" comments about other groups.

☐

☐

Directions for Using the Checklist for Planning Diversity Training

Objectives

- To plan effective diversity training.

- To evaluate training after it has been conducted so that continuous improvement can be achieved.

Intended Audience

- Trainers charged with planning and implementing diversity training.

- Planning teams, such as diversity task forces.

Time

- 30 to 45 minutes.

Training Materials

- Copies of the Checklist for Planning Diversity Training for all participants.

- Pens or pencils.

Suggested Procedures

- Ask individuals to respond to the checklist, indicating those items that have been addressed in their planning.

- If you are using it as a planning tool, those items not checked can be attended to during the training.

- If you are using it as a post-training evaluation tool, consider those items not checked and make plans for taking care of them before the next phase of training.

- If you are using the checklist with an intact group, discuss the items that were not checked and help the group make plans for ways to include them before future training.

Discussion Questions

- What aspects have been taken care of already?

- What areas have been overlooked?

- How would these omissions in planning impact our training session?

- What can be done to take care of these aspects now?

- What could be done differently next time?

Caveats and Considerations

- Although this checklist can serve as an effective self-evaluation tool for you, it is important that it not be used in a vacuum. Feedback from others, such as participants and/or co-planners, is important in order to obtain a more complete assessment.

💾 CHECKLIST FOR PLANNING DIVERSITY TRAINING

Directions: Check those conditions and actions that you have attended to in your planning.

Laying the Foundation in the Organization

_____ Diversity is seen and understood as a business imperative.

_____ There is top level understanding about how diversity connects to the organization's strategic objectives.

_____ There is commitment from the administration to making the necessary systems and policy changes.

_____ Administrators have committed to participating in diversity training.

_____ Training is one part of a larger diversity effort throughout the organization.

Pre-Planning

_____ Publicity for the training emphasizes the benefits for all attendees.

_____ Training is scheduled at the least disruptive times possible and, when feasible, options regarding which session to attend are offered.

_____ Training sites are conducive to learning.

_____ Some form of needs assessment (interviews, focus groups, questionnaire) has been conducted so that trainees' needs are clear.

_____ Necessary equipment and sufficient materials are ready and available.

_____ Participants are scheduled to attend in diverse groups.

_____ Refreshments have been arranged.

_____ Attention is paid to different needs regarding preferences and dietary laws, such as avoiding pork products for Jews and Muslims.

The Training Session Agenda

_____ The purpose and objectives are clearly communicated ahead of time to participants and reiterated at the beginning of the session.

_____ The objectives of the training are relevant to participants' needs and issues.

_____ The objectives and activities planned realistically match the time allotted.

_____ A relevant warm-up that is quick, purposeful, and focusing is planned for the beginning of the session.

_____ There are a variety of activities and groupings planned to keep people energized and involved.

_____ The agenda is structured so that participation is elicited from all attendees in some way that provides both safety and risk.

_____ Ample time is allotted for participants to process information and share reactions.

_____ Application to real, on-the-job situations is emphasized.

_____ Pairs and small groups are used to increase comfort, safety, and collegiality.

_____ Processes are structured so there is opportunity for the sharing and airing of different views.

Evaluation and Closure

_____ There is an opportunity for participants to share their insights, learnings, and "so-whats."

_____ Feedback from participants about the session is solicited.

_____ A post-session debriefing is built in so that you can conduct your own analysis of the session.

Source: Adapted from _Managing Diversity Survival Guide._ Lee Gardenswartz & Anita Rowe. Burr Ridge, IL: Irwin Professional Publishing, 1994.

Effective Diversity Training

Designing effective diversity training requires attention to both the content and process aspects of the training environment in order to create a conducive learning atmosphere and a productive session that meets the learning objectives. Certain factors must be considered in planning, whether the focus of training is awareness, knowledge, and/or skills. Each factor has strategic importance in the effectiveness of the training. They are described in the following paragraphs.

Sequence

An appropriate sequence for the learning activities is critical. Although some training content can be dealt with in separate, unrelated modules, some build on one another and are dependent on previous learning. For example, teaching participants how to conduct culturally appropriate medical interviews requires that they first understand how culture shapes behavior and then learn about the range of behaviors that exists across cultures. When designing training agendas, making sure that each activity and each concept build on the previous ones provides continuity and an environment for effective learning.

Pacing

Paying attention to energy levels and fluctuations in them is important in maintaining attention and enthusiasm. Appropriate breaks must be built in, and activities must be matched to participant energy and attention spans. For example, afternoons are generally low-energy periods, which call for more movement and active involvement. In the morning, on the other hand, most participants are more able to stay focused on lecture material.

Variety

Another way to maintain energy and attention is to vary learning experiences and modalities. Generally, a change is needed every 20 minutes. Responding to a checklist or worksheet, listening to a lecturette, watching videotaped scenarios, sharing in pairs, discussing in small groups, charting brainstormed suggestions, role playing a skill practice, or problem solving a case are examples of the different kinds of activities that can be combined to bring variety to a session.

Utilizing and varying the three learning modalities, auditory, visual, and kinesthetic, is also important. Getting participants to hear, see, and do increases the chances for learning. As the Chinese proverb tells us, "I hear and I forget; I see and I remember; I do and I know."

Grouping

The size and composition of groupings also contribute to participation and learning. In general, the smaller the grouping, the greater the comfort and motivation to participate. There is more active learner involvement in pairs than in small groups, and the least participation in large-group discussions. In addition to size of groups, consideration needs to be paid to the composition of groups. Depending on the objective of an activity, it may be more appropriate for participants to pair with someone they do not know or someone they know well, discuss an issue in a cross-departmental group, in an intact work group, or in groups by job category. Make sure there is a sound, well-thought-out reason for each grouping.

Risk

All learning involves risk. When there is no risk, there is no learning; yet when there is too much risk, participants become fearful and may balk, resist, or refuse to participate. Assessing the risk level of each activity, then sequencing activities beginning with lower risk and moving to higher risk levels is an important aspect of planning. In addition, allowing participants to control the degree of risk or self-disclosure they want to engage is helpful.

Make sure you have strategically considered these five factors as you design your training. It can pay significant dividends in minimizing resistance and increasing learning.

The PIT Model

The PIT Model[1] is an extremely effective way to sequence the workshop content. It can be used to sequence each segment of training, whether designing a two-hour executive briefing, a one-day seminar, or a three-day retreat. The model has three areas of focus:

P — Personal focus first,

I — Interpersonal focus second, and

T — Task focus third.

---

[1] Based on *PIT Meeting Model Teambook: 27 Exercises for Enhancing Work Groups.* J. E. Jones and W. L. Bearley. King of Prussia, PA: HRDQ, 1994.

The rationale for the PIT Model is that you must start with the individual in order to convey relevance. The WIFM ("What's in it for me?") principle is at work here. In order to engage employees on any issue, they have to be motivated. Relevance is a first-rate motivator.

The interpersonal focus comes next. Organizations are collective units. People need to be involved with one another a large part of the time in order to get the work done. Some work groups are interdependent; even those that are not usually require interaction. The impact of factors such as culture or stereotypes on us as team members, colleagues, or fellow staff members is important to most employees; these interpersonal dynamics ultimately impact productivity.

This leads to the third area of focus, the task itself. Ultimately, all of this training around diversity is designed to look at how staff members work together to care for patients, admit them in an efficient way, take care of their specific dietary needs, and see to it that friends and family feel comfortable visiting the institution. How diversity touches all departments, individuals, and team members in providing top notch health care is what the task focus is about.

The PIT Model should be central to the design sequence for every segment of the training session. The model provides the basis for the sample agendas we have provided on pages 43 through 47. To apply the PIT Model yourself, use the Agenda Design Worksheet on page 42 in Chapter 3 and try structuring your training segment with this model in mind.

Warm-Ups

Warm-ups serve two critical functions in any session: (1) They focus participants on the topic of the session and (2) they generate initial participation that sets the norms for active learning throughout the session. They can also be useful as an on-the-spot needs assessment of the group, giving you information about what is on participants' minds and what they hope to gain.

The warm-up needs to be short, to the point, and actively involving, that is, require participants to do something besides listen. Depending on the size of the group, the time frame of the session, and the level of risk desired, you can ask participants to respond to the whole group, share in pairs, or discuss in a small group.

The following list offers a variety of warm-up options. Have participants work in small groups or pairs and then take turns responding to selected questions or topics in the large group.

Answering Questions

- What is the good news and bad news about working on a diverse staff?

- What are the advantages and disadvantages of serving diverse patients?

- What are the biggest challenges you face in caring for diverse patients?

- What additional knowledge and skills would help you be effective in dealing with diverse patients/staff/physicians?

- If you were a member of a different group in our society (ethnicity, race, gender, physical ability, or sexual orientation), how would your experience as a patient be different? How would your professional life in this organization be different?

- What is the biggest obstacle you face in caring for patients of other cultures?

Describing Situations

- Think of a situation when you were an outsider. Describe how you felt and what helped you feel more included.

- Recall a time when you were able to overcome an intercultural communication obstacle. Describe what you did to break through the block.

- Describe an incident when you made an incorrect assumption about someone. Share the factors that led you to make that assumption.

- Share an experience in which an incorrect assumption was made about you. Describe your feelings and reactions.

- Describe a time when you were able to resolve a diversity-related conflict.

- Think of the most inclusive team or staff you have worked with. Describe the factors that made it so inclusive.

Completing Open-Ended Statements

- When I think of diversity, I think of. . . .

- I feel most effective in working with diverse patients when. . . .

- I'm most frustrated working with diverse patients when. . . .

- I feel most included at work when. . . .

- I feel most excluded on the job when. . . .
- What I like best about the way this organization deals with diversity is. . . .
- What I like least about the way this organization deals with diversity is. . . .
- The most important value to me in this organization is. . . .
- What I like best about working here is. . . .
- I feel most valued and respected as an employee here when. . . .
- I feel least valued and respected as an employee here when. . . .
- Patients feel most valued and respected here when. . . .
- Patients feel least valued and respected here when. . . .

Evaluation of Training

Measuring the impact of your training and determining whether or not its objectives have been achieved are critical aspects of the education process. Clear objectives for the training are essential for evaluation, as they serve as the targets against which results can be measured. You must decide whether the training's purpose is to stimulate awareness, to increase knowledge, and/or to build skills and competencies. In addition, baseline data must be collected so that results can be measured against pre-existing conditions and how much participants already know. Baseline data can be collected through a needs assessment questionnaire, a pre-test, and/or by using relevant organizational statistics about such aspects as patient satisfaction, grievances, and performance appraisals.

Evaluation takes place at two levels, each of which requires a different measure. The first focuses on the training process, the second on assessing the results of the training.

Evaluating the Training Process Itself

The object of evaluation at this level is to gain information about the effectiveness of the content and methods used during the sessions. Questions that need to be answered pertain to whether your objectives were met, as well as what worked and what did not. Some sample questions follow:

- How relevant and applicable to participants' jobs was the content?
- How comfortable and inviting was the learning environment?

- How involving and stimulating were the learning activities and processes?

- How clear, interesting, and stimulating was the trainer?

- What did participants learn?

- Where will they apply or use what they have learned?

Data can be collected in answer to this type of question at the close of the session by using an evaluation form that participants fill out before leaving. Generally, using a scale (with 1 as low and 5 as high) elicits a higher response rate than open-ended questions that require participants to write out their answers.

Evaluating Results of Training

The second area requiring evaluation pertains to results. You need to know what the outcome of the training was and how it benefitted or impacted the organization. Some samples of the kinds of questions that need to be answered at this level follow:

- How are trainees applying their learning on the job?

- How does their newly acquired knowledge or skill impact organizational productivity, quality of care, and patient service, as well as teamwork, communication, and employee satisfaction?

- What is the return on investment (ROI) for the organization?

Data can be collected to answer these types of questions approximately three to six months after the training through a survey of trainees and/or their immediate supervisors. Pre- and post-measures of patient satisfaction, output, and employee satisfaction or before and after performance evaluations can also be used. It is important to remember when evaluating training that it does not take place in a vacuum; many other variables within the organization may influence both the results and the data that are collected. When collecting data, use control groups that have not participated in the training for comparison to isolate the effects of training. This limits any confusion and produces more accurate measures.

Chapter 3

Structuring Agendas Using the Activities in this Book

PART TWO OF THIS BOOK contains myriad training activities for helping health care staff members deal effectively with diversity. They are grouped in chapters by topic area, and many activities have similar objectives. This gives you, the trainer, maximum flexibility in designing training interventions and agendas. It also gives you numerous options from which to choose. By using your knowledge of the trainees, the organization, and the environment in which they work, as well as the design guidelines presented in this and subsequent chapters, you can structure the most appropriate training program for your needs.

First, look at the Agenda Design Sheet section that follows and then fill out an Agenda Design Worksheet for your own training.

The five sample agendas that follow provide models of how activities can be chosen and sequenced to suit specific objectives, groups, and time constraints. They are not intended to be used as templates, but rather as *examples* that integrate the design principles with the variety of activities in the second part of this workbook.

Agenda Design Worksheet

Introductions

Decide who needs to be introduced, for example, participants, speakers, trainers, members of upper management, or someone from the organization who will bless and legitimize the session.

Introductions should be brief, but relevant. They should build credibility for speakers, as well as give a clear and compelling rationale for why participants are present.

Objectives

This should be an uncomplicated statement of desired outcomes for this particular session. Some sample objectives are listed below.

Participants will:

- Learn about demographic trends in our community for the next ten years.

- Gain ways to communicate more effectively with patients from other cultures.

- Discuss and explore the impact of changing demographics on our medical center.

Display the objectives on an easel chart, overhead projector, or slide projector. Discuss them in some depth; do not just read them. Provide a context for the objectives by explaining how they are part of a long-term process and by giving the long-range goals of the effort.

Warm-Up

For more in-depth information about warm-ups, see Chapter 2. A sample warm-up for the last objective listed above might be:

- What are the biggest demographic changes you have noticed in the last year?

- What changes have you seen over the past five years?

- What words would you use to describe the impact of these changes?

Activities

The next item on your agenda should be the centerpiece for the concept you are teaching. Again, look at the five sample agendas on the following pages. Use the guidelines regarding sequencing, pace, and variety as you select relevant activities to construct your own agenda. Choose from the many activities in Part II to fill the bill.

Closure

A formal closing helps participants bring the learning activity to a close and decide on applications. Some sample questions to ask might be:

- What will you do differently the next time you serve a patient of a different background?

- What is your most important learning from this session and where will you apply it?

⊞ AGENDA DESIGN WORKSHEET

Directions: Fill out the worksheet below using the PIT Model whenever possible. Feel free to reproduce and use this worksheet for future planning.

Introduction (Why, Who, What)

- P

- I

- T

Objectives

- P

- I

- T

Warm-Up

- P

- I

- T

Activities

- P

- I

- T

Closure

- P

- I

- T

Next Steps

Next Steps

Decide whether you need to set times for follow-up meetings. Have you given participants any homework or follow-up work with their supervisors? If you set dates for follow-up, be sure to have a communication system to remind people of them and that someone is responsible for implementing any follow-up.

Use the Agenda Design Worksheet on the facing page to apply these guidelines and structure an agenda for your training session incorporating the PIT Model discussed earlier.

SAMPLE AGENDA 1:
EXECUTIVE BRIEFING
UNDERSTANDING DIVERSITY'S IMPACT

Executive Staff (2 Hours)

Time	Activity	Process
5 min	**Introduction and Purpose**	Lecturette
5 min	**Objectives:** ♦ To gain information about diversity. ♦ To discuss its impact on the organization/hospital/medical center. ♦ To determine next steps in dealing with diversity.	Lecturette
20 min	**Warm-Up:** **"Changing Demographics"** (2 worksheets) (Chapter 4)	Worksheets, answers on sheet or overhead, large group discussion
15 min	**"Effects of Increased Diversity"** (2 worksheets) (Chapter 4)	Worksheets, charting of responses, and large group discussion
30 min	**"The Four Layers of Diversity"** (Chapter 2, *Managing Diversity in Health Care*)	Lecturette
30 min	**"Assessing the Impact of Diversity in Your Health Care Organization"** (Chapter 5)	Worksheet, large group discussion
10 min	**Next Steps in Dealing with Diversity**	Large group discussion
5 min	**Summary**	Lecturette

SAMPLE AGENDA 2:
DIVERSITY AWARENESS
All Staff (7 Hours)

Time	Activity	Process
5 min	**Introduction and Purpose**	Lecturette
20 min	**Warm-Up:** • The biggest changes I've seen in the past two years … • Among staff • Among patients	Individual response or paired sharing
5 min	**Objectives:** • To increase awareness about diversity and its impact. • To gain information about cultural differences. • To enhance ability to deal with differences.	Lecturette
30 min	**"Effects of Increased Diversity"** (2 worksheets) (Chapter 4)	Worksheets, small group discussion
30 min	**"The Four Layers of Diversity"** (Chapter 2, *Managing Diversity in Health Care*)	Lecturette
30 min	**"Assessing the Impact of Diversity in Your Health Care Organization"** (Chapter 5)	Worksheet, small group discussion
15 min	**Break**	
45 min	**"Analyzing Your Own Cultural 'Software' "** (Chapter 6)	Lecturette, worksheet, paired sharing
45 min	**"Aspects of Culture"** (Chapter 6)	Lecturette, large group discussion
30 min	**"Expanding Cultural Interpretations"** (Chapter 6)	Worksheet, paired sharing
60 min	**Lunch**	
15 min	**Energizer** What stereotypes come to mind when you hear … (List three or four labels that generate interest in group such as surgeons, immigrants, Medicaid patients)	Total group brainstorming/ charting
30 min	**"Understanding Stereotypes"** (Chapter 6, *Managing Diversity in Health Care*)	Lecturette
45 min	**"You As the Object of Stereotypes"** (Chapter 9)	Worksheet, paired sharing
45 min	**"Assumptions: What You See Is What You Get"** (Chapter 9)	Worksheet, small group sharing
15 min	**Break**	
45 min	**"Comments and Behaviors That May Indicate Stereotypes and Prejudice in Your Hospital or Medical Center"** (Chapter 9)	Worksheet, small group discussion
20 min	**Brainstorming Suggested Approaches to Stereotypes and Prejudice**	Small group problem solving and charting, reporting to whole group
10 min	**Summary and Closure:** • Biggest insight/learning from this session. or • One thing I'll do differently in dealing with diversity.	Individual response or paired sharing

SAMPLE AGENDA 3:
MANAGING CULTURAL DIFFERENCES
Managers ($3\frac{1}{2}$ Hours)

Time	Activity	Process
5 min	**Introduction and Purpose** Why this class; credentials of trainer; introduction of participants.	Lecturette
10 min	**Warm-Up:** • What do we do best as an organization to demonstrate a welcome to people of all cultures? • What is one thing we need to do better to make everyone feel welcome and comfortable?	Have people pair up and discuss. Then, depending on size of group, obtain either total or random responses and chart.
5 min	**Objectives:** • To stimulate discussion about essential behaviors necessary for employees in a cross-cultural health care environment. • To increase cultural understanding and improve relationships. • To identify signs of a diversity-friendly organization. • To define some clear behaviors that managers can teach their staff. • To offer suggestions and behaviors for becoming more diversity friendly toward fellow staff members and patients/family.	Lecturette
20 min	**"Culture as Software"** (Chapter 3, *Managing Diversity in Health Care*) **"An Overall Glance at Key Cultural Values and How They Impact Care"** (Chapter 7) (Chapter 4, *Managing Diversity in Health Care*)	Lecturette Distribute worksheets and conduct total group discussion, providing time for questions and answers
35 min	**"Key Cultural Values Impacting Care"** (Chapter 7)	Worksheet, small group discussion
15 min	**Break**	
40 min	**"Serving Diverse Patients and Families:** **An Assessment Questionnaire"** (Chapter 11)	Questionnaire, small group discussion, followed by total group discussion
50 min	**"Behaviors of an Effective Health Care Employee in a Pluralistic Environment"** (Chapter 11)	Worksheet, small group activity, then large group discussion focusing on how to use this tool for each employee and generate discussion
20 min	**Expanding Cultural Interpretations** (Chapter 6)	Worksheet, paired sharing
10 min	**Summary and Closure** • One behavior I will interpret differently is ... or • One way I can respond more effectively to a patient of a different culture is ...	Individual responses or paired sharing

SAMPLE AGENDA 4:
CULTURAL DIFFERENCES IN PATIENT CARE

Patient Care Staff ($3\frac{1}{2}$ Hours)

Time	Activity	Process
10 min	**Introduction and Purpose** Welcome and introduction of trainer and all participants	Lecturette
15 min	**Warm-Up:** What patient and family norms, traditions, or practices are either • Hard for you to deal with? • Confusing? • Anxiety producing? • Irritating?	Discuss at tables and then solicit random responses and chart; use data to lead into objectives
5 min	**Objectives:** • To assess diversity friendliness of the organization. • To understand a broad array of cultural norms as they relate to health care. • To expand comfort and competence with a wide range of norms.	Lecturette
20 min	**"Culture as Software"** (Chapter 3, *Managing Diversity in Health Care*)	Lecturette
40 min	**"How Culturally Sensitive Are You?"** (Chapter 7)	Individual assessment worksheet, paired sharing, followed by total group discussion of what this data implies for the health care organization
15 min	**Break**	
45 min	**"Intercultural Hooks That Block Communication"** (Chapter 8)	Individual assessment worksheet, small group problem solving on most common hooks, report out to all
45 min	**"Cultural Differences Affecting Communication with Patients and Staff"** (Chapter 8)	Individual assessment discussion at tables, followed by total group application discussion
15 min	**Summary and Closure** One thing I will do differently with patients of other backgrounds in the future is ...	Trainer summarizes, each participant responds

SAMPLE AGENDA 5:
COMMUNICATING ACROSS CULTURES

Patient Service Staff ($3\frac{1}{2}$ Hours)

Time	Activity	Process
5 min	**Introduction and Purpose**	Lecturette
5 min	**Objectives:** • To identify and understand cultural differences influencing communication. • To gain skills and approaches to increase effectiveness in cross-cultural communication.	Lecturette
20 min	**"Language and You"** (Chapter 8)	Paired sharing
30 min	**"Intercultural Hooks That Block Communication"** (Chapter 8)	Worksheet, small group discussion
45 min	**"Cultural Differences Affecting Communication with Patients and Staff"** (Chapter 8) (Chapter 5 in *Managing Diversity in Health Care*)	Lecturette, worksheet, paired sharing
15 min	**Break**	
15 min	**"Communicating Across Language Barriers"** (Chapter 8) (Chapter 5 in *Managing Diversity in Health Care*)	Lecturette, worksheet
30 min	**"Giving Directions and Explanations in Culturally Sensitive Ways"** (Chapter 8) (Chapter 5 in *Managing Diversity in Health Care*)	Lecturette, worksheet, paired sharing
40 min	**"Practice in Conducting Culturally Sensitive Medical Interviews: Using the LEARN Steps"** (Chapter 8)	Lecturette, Triad role play
5 min	**Summary and Closure** One thing I'll do next time communication with a patient is blocked is …	Paired sharing

Part Two
Learning Activities

PART TWO PROVIDES A SERIES OF TRAINING ACTIVITIES that are grouped by content areas that correspond to the content areas in *Managing Diversity in Health Care.* Lecturette and handout information to support the learning activities are found in the indicated chapters. Each activity is carefully structured to accomplish specific objectives. Because many of the learning activities are designed to accomplish similar objectives, the trainer has many options from which to select appropriate learning activities for any audience, educational level, and purpose, as well as to suit his or her own preferences for different learning modes.

Chapter 4
Why Diversity Is Good for Business

BETTER MANAGEMENT OF STAFF DIVERSITY as well as diversity of patients and their families is not just the right thing to do from an ethical perspective, but it is good for business. Helping participants understand this practical reality is an important aspect of diversity training. A pragmatic approach emphasizes increasing effectiveness in delivering care and ensures the financial viability of the health care institution. The following activities provide ways to engage participants in discussing and considering the business implications of diversity.

Also see Chapter 1 in *Managing Diversity in Health Care* for further content information to support the activities.

Directions for Using Either Changing Demographics Sheet

Objectives
- To increase awareness about demographic realities of the patient and/or employee base.
- To encourage investigation of demographic changes and their impact on the workplace.
- To stimulate discussion about demographic changes and their implications.

Intended Audience
- Executives leading diverse health care organizations.
- Managers of diverse staffs and of direct service units or departments.
- Employees working on diverse staffs or serving diverse patients.

Time
- 30 minutes per form.

Materials
- Copies of Changing Demographics: Do You Know Your Patients? and/or Changing Demographics: Do You Know Your Workforce? for all participants.

- Pens or pencils.

- Demographic facts and figures for your workforce and/or service area prepared and presented on an overhead transparency or as a handout.

Suggested Procedures
- As pre-work, gather information to complete the form(s) to be used.

- Ask participants to respond to the worksheet, estimating the percentage in each category.

- Then reveal the correct answers by showing a transparency or distributing a handout.

- Have participants compare their responses with your answers.

- Lead a total group discussion of surprises, insights, and implications.

Discussion Questions
- Where were you most accurate? What was your biggest misperception?

- On what information did you base your estimates or responses?

- What data surprised you?

- What implications does this information have for our institution/organization?

Caveats, Considerations, and Adaptations
- You may need to adjust categories to suit your institution and its demographics by adding certain languages or ethnic groups to the forms.

- You may also shorten the activity, using only those categories that are most important or striking, for example, just focusing on how many and which languages are the native languages of staff or patients.

- This activity requires pre-work to gather the appropriate demographic data and prepare overheads or handout sheets.

💾 CHANGING DEMOGRAPHICS: DO YOU KNOW YOUR PATIENTS?

Directions: Estimate the percentage of your facility's patients in each category below.

General Information

Household Income	Under $20,000		$20,000–$35,000
	$35,000–$50,000		Over $50,000
Age	20–35	36–49	50+
Gender	Male	Female	
Marital Status	Married	Single	Single Parent
Average number of children			

Ethnic Group

African-American	Latino	Filipino
Korean	Armenian	Chinese
Indian	Japanese	Middle Eastern
Russian	Native American	Euro-American
Vietnamese	Laotian	Cambodian
Haitian	Other	

Educational Level

Elementary School	Some High School	High School Diploma
Some College	Trade School	College Graduate
Advanced Degree		

Languages Spoken

English	Spanish	Russian	Korean
Tagalog	Mandarin	Vietnamese	French
Cantonese	Cambodian	Laotian	Farsi
Limited or non-English speaking	Bilingual		
Other languages spoken			

🖫 CHANGING DEMOGRAPHICS: DO YOU KNOW YOUR WORKFORCE?

Directions: Estimate the percentage of your facility's workforce in each category below.

General Information

Household Income	Under $20,000		$20,000–$35,000
	$35,000–$50,000		Over $50,000
Age	20–35	36–49	50+
Gender	Male	Female	
Marital Status	Married	Single	Single Parent
Average number of children			

Ethnic Group

African-American	Latino	Filipino
Korean	Armenian	Chinese
Indian	Japanese	Middle Eastern
Russian	Native American	Euro-American
Vietnamese	Laotian	Cambodian
Haitian	Other	

Educational Level

Elementary School	Some High School	High School Diploma
Some College	Trade School	College Graduate
Advanced Degree		

Languages Spoken

English	Spanish	Russian	Korean
Tagalog	Mandarin	Vietnamese	French
Cantonese	Cambodian	Laotian	Farsi
Limited or non-English speaking	Bilingual		
Other languages spoken			

Directions for Using Either Effects of Increased Diversity Worksheet

Objectives

- To stimulate discussion of the positive and negative effects of increased diversity.

- To increase understanding of the business case for addressing diversity.

- To bring balance to the discussion of diversity and its impact.

Intended Audience

- Participants in diversity awareness training.

- Staff attending a diversity briefing or information session.

- Employees working on a diverse staff or serving diverse patients and families.

Time

- 30 minutes per worksheet

Materials

- Copies of the Effects of Increased Diversity in the Workplace and/or the Effects of Increased Diversity in the Patient Base worksheet for all participants.

- Pens or pencils.

- Easel and newsprint pad.

- Felt-tipped markers.

Suggested Procedures

- Begin by asking participants about the biggest changes they have seen in the workforce and patient base in the past few years.

- Present demographic information about changes in the workforce and patient base in the service area.

- Explain that all changes cut two ways, bringing both challenges and opportunities.

- Ask participants to respond to the worksheet, listing challenges and opportunities they have already experienced, as well as those they anticipate experiencing in the future.

- Have participants form small groups (five or six people) and share responses; chart their collective data.

- Have each group select the two or three most significant opportunities that need to be taken advantage of and two or three most critical challenges that need to be dealt with.

- Ask a reporter from each group to share the group's top priority opportunities and challenges.

- Lead a total group discussion of themes and issues.

Discussion Questions
- What challenges and opportunities do you have in common?

- What additional ones did you become aware of during this session?

- What are the most significant opportunities?

- What needs to be done to take advantage of them?

- What are the most critical challenges?

- What needs to be done to deal with them?

- What would happen if we did nothing in response to these changes?

Caveats, Considerations, and Adaptations
- If the group is small, you may lead the total group in charting and discussing trends, rather than breaking up into small groups.

- The two activities can be combined, dealing with both the workforce and patient base on the same worksheet.

🖫 EFFECTS OF INCREASED DIVERSITY
IN THE WORKFORCE

Directions: Consider the existing and potential impact of increased diversity in the workforce. List both the challenges and obstacles, as well as the opportunities and benefits it brings for you, your work group, and your organization.

	Challenges and Obstacles	Opportunities and Benefits
For Me		
For My Department/ Unit/Team		
For the Hospital/ Clinic/Agency		

🖫 EFFECTS OF INCREASED DIVERSITY
IN THE PATIENT BASE

Directions: Consider the existing and potential impact of increased diversity in the patient base. List both the challenges and obstacles, as well as the opportunities and benefits it brings for you, your work group, and your organization.

	Challenges and Obstacles	Opportunities and Benefits
For Me		
For My Department/ Unit/Team		
For the Hospital/ Clinic/Agency		

Chapter 5

The Dimensions of Health Care Diversity

A FUNDAMENTAL ASPECT OF DIVERSITY TRAINING involves an awareness of the many dimensions of diversity. Understanding how these factors influence the behavior and life situations of both staff and patients in a health care setting is a critical underpinning of dealing effectively with differences. The following activities offer many approaches that help participants consider the impact of diversity and gain understanding of both themselves and others. Further information on the concepts underlying these activities can be found in Chapter 2 of *Managing Diversity in Health Care.*

First have participants examine the model of the four layers of diversity on the following page.

Directions for Using the Four Layers of Diversity and Assessing the Impact of Diversity in Your Health Care Organization

Objectives

- To increase understanding about the dimensions of diversity.

- To raise awareness about the impact of these dimensions on treatment of staff and patients.

- To open discussion and share perceptions regarding the impact of diversity.

Intended Audience

- Participants in diversity awareness training.

- Members of diverse work groups.

- Managers of diverse teams.
- Staff serving diverse patients.
- Executives leading diverse organizations.

Time
- 60 minutes.

Materials
- Copies of the Four Layers of Diversity and Assessing the Impact of Diversity in Your Health Care Organization for all participants.
- Pens and pencils.
- Easels and newsprint paper.

Suggested Procedures
- Give a brief lecturette on the Four Layers of Diversity, giving and soliciting examples. (See Chapter 2 in *Managing Diversity in Health Care.*) Distribute copies if desired.
- Distribute the worksheet and ask participants to consider the impact of each dimension of diversity on the job by responding to the worksheet. Emphasize that there are no "right" answers, but that each person's perceptions are important and valid.
- Have participants gather in small groups (four to six people) and share their responses, focusing on those high-impact dimensions that seem to pose the biggest obstacles to full inclusion, as well as on those dimensions on which their scores seem to vary greatly.
- Lead a total group discussion of issues and insights.

Discussion Questions
- Which dimensions seem to make the most difference in how staff are treated? Patients?
- How are those differences in treatment shown?
- On what dimensions are there variations in ratings among group members?
- What did you learn from other group members' perceptions?
- To what do you attribute these differences in perception?
- What are the consequences of these differences in treatment for the organization in areas such as morale, teamwork, productivity, patient satisfaction, and patient care?

Caveats, Considerations, and Adaptations

- Poster-sized enlarged copies of the worksheet may be made and posted on the wall for small-group discussion. Group members can then mark their ratings on the posted chart to see a visual representation of the group's composite ratings.

- You can chart the top three high-impact areas from each group on an easel in front of the room prior to the discussion.

- This tool can also be used as a needs assessment, identifying problem areas in the organization or work group.

- Participants may disagree about ratings. It is important to reiterate that all perceptions are valid and that the purpose of this activity is to identify problem areas and to listen and learn from others' experiences and perceptions.

- This activity may be shortened by directing participants to select only the three most impactful dimensions (after considering all of them), rather than rating each one separately.

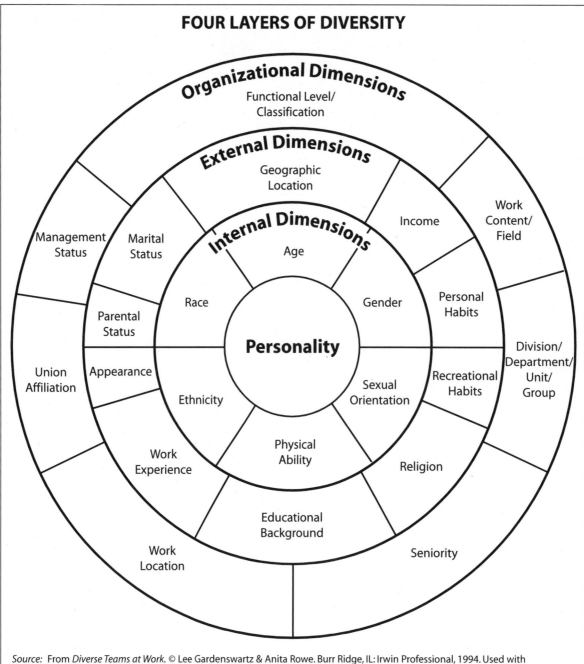

FOUR LAYERS OF DIVERSITY

Source: From *Diverse Teams at Work.* © Lee Gardenswartz & Anita Rowe. Burr Ridge, IL: Irwin Professional, 1994. Used with permission.

Note: Internal Dimensions and External Dimensions are adapted from Marilyn Loden and Judy Rosener, *Workforce America!* Burr Ridge, IL: Irwin Professional, 1991.

💾 ASSESSING THE IMPACT OF DIVERSITY IN YOUR HEALTH CARE ORGANIZATION

Directions: Think about each dimension of diversity and rate the degree of difference each makes in how people are treated in your health care organization. Mark an **"S"** indicating the degree of difference this dimension makes in how staff are treated and a **"P"** for how much difference it makes with regard to how patients are treated. (Note: the organizational dimensions may not be relevant for patients.)

	1 Little difference	2 Minor difference	3 Some difference	4 Much difference	5 Great deal of difference
Personality					
Different styles and characteristics					
Internal Dimensions					
Age					
Gender					
Sexual Orientation					
Physical Ability					
Ethnicity					
Race					
External Dimensions					
Geographic Location					
Income					
Personal Habits					
Recreational Habits					
Religion					
Educational Background					
Work Experience					
Appearance					
Parental Status					
Marital Status					
Organizational Dimensions					
Functional Level/Classification					
Work Content/Field					
Division/Department/Unit/Group					
Seniority					
Work Location					
Union Affiliation					
Management Status					

Source: Adapted from *Diverse Teams at Work,* © Lee Gardenswartz and Anita Rowe. Burr Ridge, IL: Irwin Professional, 1995. Used with permission.

Directions for Using Analyzing the Influence of Your Own Diversity on You as a Health Care Professional

Objectives

- To identify the impact of diversity on one's professional life and behavior.

- To increase awareness of the complexity of and interrelationships among diversity dimensions.

- To learn more about co-workers in order to increase understanding and develop common ground.

Intended Audience

- Participants in diversity awareness training.

- Members of a diverse work group.

- Managers of diverse teams.

- Staff who serve diverse patients and family members.

Time

- 45 minutes.

Materials

- Copies of Analyzing the Influence of Your Own Diversity on You As a Health Care Professional for all participants.

- Pens and pencils.

- Easel and newsprint paper with the example drawn on it.

Suggested Procedures

- Acquaint participants with the Four Layers of Diversity.

- Introduce the activity by explaining that we are all products of the many dimensions of our own diversity. These aspects of our development influence our behavior and interactions on the job daily. As health care professionals it is critical to understand these influences in order to make proactive choices about our own behavior.

- Give examples of diversity dimensions and their influence on your own professional life by charting examples on the easel.

- Tell participants to fill out their own worksheets, noting the most significant dimension in each category, and the impact it has had on them professionally.

- Pair participants, preferably with someone they do not know well, and ask them to share their responses, focusing on similarities and differences and on learning about one another.

- Lead a total group discussion of reactions, insights, learning, and applications.

Discussion Questions

- Which dimensions were most important for your development?

- What has been their impact on your life and career?

- What surprises did you find?

- What similarities and differences did you find with your partner?

- What insights did you have?

- What do you know about how the diversity dimensions have influenced your co-workers, supervisors, and patients? How can you learn more?

- What does this tell you about dealing with others who are different from you?

- How will you apply your learning or insight from this activity?

Caveats, Considerations, and Adaptations

- This activity causes participants to reflect on childhood, which can be a painful or emotional experience for some. It is not unusual to see tear-filled eyes as individuals share memories and experiences.

- Tell participants at the beginning of the activity that they will be sharing their responses with another person in the room. In this way, individuals can control the degree of disclosure and risk.

⊞ ANALYZING THE INFLUENCE OF YOUR OWN DIVERSITY ON YOU AS A HEALTH CARE PROFESSIONAL

Directions: Select the most important dimension for your own development from each of the four layers of diversity, for example, age from Internal Dimensions, marital status from External Dimensions, and functional level from Organizational Dimensions. Then think about the influence of each of those dimensions and the impact that each has had on your life and work as a health care professional. (See the example on the next page.)

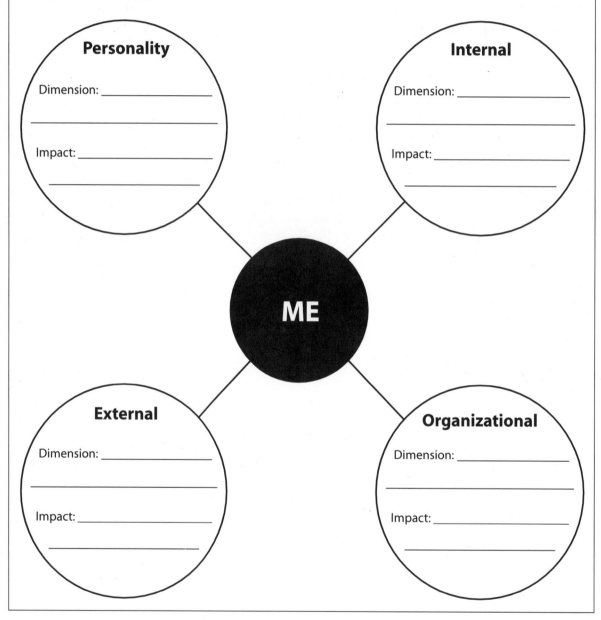

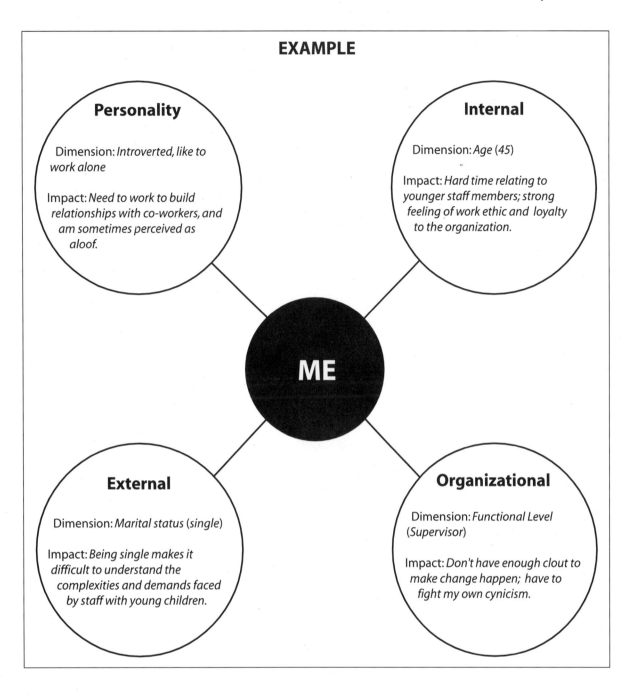

EXAMPLE

Personality

Dimension: *Introverted, like to work alone*

Impact: *Need to work to build relationships with co-workers, and am sometimes perceived as aloof.*

Internal

Dimension: *Age (45)*

Impact: *Hard time relating to younger staff members; strong feeling of work ethic and loyalty to the organization.*

ME

External

Dimension: *Marital status (single)*

Impact: *Being single makes it difficult to understand the complexities and demands faced by staff with young children.*

Organizational

Dimension: *Functional Level (Supervisor)*

Impact: *Don't have enough clout to make change happen; have to fight my own cynicism.*

Directions for Using Assumptions About Appearance

Objectives

- To raise awareness about one's own assumptions and biases.

- To question accepted assumptions about appearance.

- To increase acceptance and understanding of those who are different.

Intended Audience

- Participants in diversity awareness training.

- Managers of staff who serve diverse patients and family members.

- Staff who serve diverse patients and family members.

Time

- 45 minutes.

Materials

- Copies of the Assumptions About Appearance worksheet for everyone.

- Pens or pencils.

- Easel with newsprint paper.

- Felt-tipped markers.

Suggested Procedures

- Introduce the topic by asking for reactions to the old adage, "Don't judge a book by its cover."

- Also ask a few participants to share examples of times when incorrect assumptions were made about them based solely on appearance or when they made incorrect assumptions based on the appearance of another person.

- Ask participants to brainstorm appearance "turnoffs."

- Tell participants to fill out their own worksheets, listing assumptions for any of the appearance factors that they would react to, and indicating whether their reaction would be positive, negative, or neutral.

- Group participants in pairs or threesomes and ask them to share their assumptions and reactions.

- Tell participants to attempt to expand their thinking by challenging one another's assumptions and by finding additional ways to view the various appearance factors. (For example, a facial veil does not necessarily mean a woman is submissive and subjugated; dreadlocks do not necessarily indicate radical militancy; nor is a business suit the mark of an upstanding citizen.)

- Lead a total group discussion of insights, learnings, and applications.

Discussion Questions

- What assumptions did you make based on appearance?

- Which did you have in common with your partner(s)?

- Where do these assumptions come from?

- Which are hardest to change?

- What are the consequences of these assumptions on your interactions with the individual you are observing?

- What new interpretations were you able to see?

- What insights did you have regarding your own and others' reactions to appearance?

- What can you do the next time you make assumptions based on appearance?

Caveats, Considerations, and Adaptations

- Participants may be reluctant to question their assumptions. If this is the case, then ask them what they gain by hanging on to them. Assure them that they do not need to discard old assumptions, but rather to question the accuracy of their assumptions by considering other possible interpretations of these appearance factors.

- To shorten the activity, ask participants to select only the three appearance factors that would stimulate the biggest reactions from them.

- Asking participants to brainstorm appearance "turnoffs" could, in some groups, be volatile. To make it less so, ask participants to list their own "turnoffs" privately and to share their lists in a paired discussion.

💾 ASSUMPTIONS ABOUT APPEARANCE

Directions: Jot down the assumptions you would make about an employee or patient with any of the following appearance/grooming factors. Then indicate if that assumption would have a positive, negative, or neutral impact on your interaction with that person.

Dress/Grooming Factor	Assumptions	Impact +, −, or Neutral
• Tattoo		
• Shaved head		
• Pierced nose, tongue, or eyebrow		
• Dreadlocks		
• Turban		
• Yarmulke		
• Head scarf (male)		
• Head scarf (female)		
• Facial veil		
• Lab coat		
• Military uniform		
• Police uniform		
• Business suit		
• Sweat suit		
• Unnatural hair color (e.g., green, purple)		
• Ethnic dress		
• Dyed hair		
• Wig/toupee		
•		

Directions for Using Checking Your Own Comfort with Differences

Objectives

- To raise awareness about discomfort with differences.
- To increase understanding about and comfort with differences.

Intended Audience

- Participants in diversity awareness training.
- Members of diverse work groups.
- Managers of diverse teams and direct service departments.
- Staff who serve diverse patients and family members.

Time

- 45 minutes.

Materials

- Copies of the Checking Your Own Comfort with Differences worksheet for all participants.
- Pens or pencils.

Suggested Procedures

- Introduce the activity by asking participants to think of people at work with whom they feel most and least comfortable. Lead a short discussion of the differences between the most comfortable and least comfortable and what factors are involved (for example, similar values, common interests, or different educational levels).
- Tell participants to fill out the worksheet, indicating level of comfort or discomfort with staff and patients different from them on various dimensions.
- Tell participants they will be sharing their responses with others in small groups.
- Group participants in pairs, threesomes, or small groups to discuss ratings, their reasons, and the consequences.
- Lead a total group debriefing of the activity.

Discussion Questions

- Around which dimensions was there most comfort? Least comfort?
- What differences are there between staff and patient ratings?
- To what do you attribute the discomfort?

- What is the consequence of a high degree of comfort? Discomfort?

- What have you done or can you do in the future to increase comfort with differences?

- What is one action you can take to increase your comfort with those different from you?

Caveats, Considerations, and Adaptations

- This activity requires a great deal of self-disclosure. Because of the high risk level, it should not be attempted until a foundation has been laid and trust has been built in the group with the use of lower risk disclosure activities.

- To decrease the risk, participants can choose their own partners for sharing or can share in pairs rather than small groups.

- If sharing dimensions that cause discomfort seems too risky, participants can do the activity individually and then only share one action step they plan to take to become more comfortable with staff or patients different on a particular dimension, without revealing that dimension.

💾 CHECKING YOUR OWN COMFORT WITH DIFFERENCES

Directions: Circle the number representing your degree of comfort with staff different from you in each dimension. Put a square around the numbers representing your degree of comfort with patients different from you in each dimension. (Note: Organizational dimensions may not be relevant for patients.)

	Degree of Comfort				
Dimensions	**Very Uncomfortable**	**Uncomfortable**	**Somewhat Comfortable**	**Comfortable**	**Very Comfortable**
Personality	1	2	3	4	5
Internal Dimensions					
Age	1	2	3	4	5
Gender	1	2	3	4	5
Sexual Orientation	1	2	3	4	5
Physical Ability	1	2	3	4	5
Ethnicity	1	2	3	4	5
Race	1	2	3	4	5
External Dimensions					
Geographic Location	1	2	3	4	5
Income	1	2	3	4	5
Personal Habits	1	2	3	4	5
Recreational Habits	1	2	3	4	5
Religion	1	2	3	4	5
Educational Background	1	2	3	4	5
Work Experience	1	2	3	4	5
Appearance	1	2	3	4	5
Parental Status	1	2	3	4	5
Marital Status	1	2	3	4	5
Organizational Dimensions					
Functional Level/ Classification	1	2	3	4	5
Work Content/Field	1	2	3	4	5
Division/Department/ Unit/Group	1	2	3	4	5
Seniority	1	2	3	4	5
Work Location	1	2	3	4	5
Union Affiliation	1	2	3	4	5
Management Status	1	2	3	4	5

Chapter 6

The Truth About Cultural Programming

CULTURE HAS BEEN LIKENED TO SOFTWARE that programs our behavior. An essential step in dealing with diversity is to understand the powerful role that cultural programming plays in interactions between staff members and between staff and patients and families. Understanding one's own cultural software and recognizing the wide range of norms, values, and preferences that exists across cultures helps participants to respond less ethnocentrically and to keep from misinterpreting others' behavior. This broadened understanding also positions staff to be more effective cross-cultural problem solvers.

Content information that supports the activities in this chapter is found in Chapter 3 of *Managing Diversity in Health Care*.

Directions for Using Analyzing Your Own Cultural "Software"

Objectives
- To increase understanding of the influence of one's own cultural programming.
- To build awareness that others have different cultural programming.
- To build common ground with co-workers of different backgrounds.

Intended Audience
- Participants in diversity awareness training.
- Members of diverse work groups.

- Managers of diverse teams or departments.
- Staff serving diverse patients and family members.

Time
- 45 to 60 minutes.

Materials
- Copies of the Analyzing Your Own Cultural "Software" worksheet for all participants.
- Pens or pencils.
- Easel with newsprint paper.
- Felt-tipped markers.

Suggested Procedures
- Give a short lecturette explaining that culture is like a software program that directs our behavior, using a few examples to illustrate the point. (See Chapter 3 in *Managing Diversity in Health Care*.)
- Ask participants to brainstorm sources of their own software, charting participants' responses, as well as the values or norms learned from each source, on the newsprint pad.
- Have participants delineate their own software influences by filling out the worksheet.
- Explain that participants will be sharing their responses with another individual in the next phase of the activity.
- Tell participants to pair up, preferably with someone they do not know well and who is different from them on some diversity dimensions. Tell them to share information with their partners about the development of their own cultural software and its impact on their lives.
- Lead a total group debriefing discussion focusing on insights and applications.

Discussion Questions
- What similarities and differences were there in your software programs?
- Were there any surprises?
- What were the most important influences on your beliefs and values?

- What changes have you seen in your values and beliefs over the years?

- Where do values and beliefs from one source conflict with those from another?

- How do you resolve those differences?

- How do these beliefs and values impact your work?

- What insight does this give you about working in a diverse environment?

- How can this insight help you on the job?

Caveats, Considerations, and Adaptations

- Because this activity requires a look into the past, it may dredge up some painful memories or experiences. Let participants know ahead of time that they will be asked to share information about this. Also, explain that not all influences are positive and that negative ones also play a role in the development of our software.

💾 ANALYZING YOUR OWN CULTURAL "SOFTWARE"

Directions: Think of the most important influences on the development of your individual cultural "software" program. Using those already listed that pertain and adding others, list the most significant values, norms, rules, and beliefs you have adopted from each source. Then indicate what impact each has made on your life and work. For example, if your parents taught you the value of a strong work ethic, does that make you a responsible and conscientious employee? Does it also make you impatient with co-workers who don't work as hard or frustrated with patients who receive public assistance?

Source	Values, Rules, Norms, Beliefs Adopted	Impact on Life and Work
Family 　　Parents 　　Siblings 　　Grandparents 　　Extended family 　　Spouse 　　Children		
Geographic Location 　　Country 　　Neighborhood 　　Childhood 　　Present residence		
Religion 　　Early years 　　Currently		
Education 　　School 　　College/University 　　Continuing		
Friends 　　Childhood 　　Current 　　Colleagues/Co-workers		
Professional Life 　　Field of work		
Other		

Directions for Using Aspects of Culture: Their Impact in a Health Care Setting

Objectives

- To recognize the cultural roots of behaviors encountered at work.

- To expand understanding and knowledge of different cultural norms.

- To stimulate thinking about additional ways to meet a wider range of needs and preferences.

Intended Audience

- Participants in diversity training.

- Managers of diverse staffs and of direct service departments or units.

- Employees dealing with individuals (staff, patients, physicians, family members) from other cultures.

Time

- 60 minutes.

Materials

- Copies of the Aspects of Culture worksheet for all participants.

- Pens or pencils.

- Easel with newsprint pad.

- Felt-tipped markers.

Suggested Procedures

- Give an interactive lecturette on the range of norms in the ten aspects of culture. (See Chapters 3 and 4 in *Managing Diversity in Health Care.*) Ask participants to contribute examples and make notes on their worksheets.

- Divide the participants into small groups, with each discussing one, two, or three of the areas of programming, sharing differences and their impact in health care settings.

- Have each group make a chart of the group's brainstormed adaptations the institution could make to meet these different needs or preferences.

- Ask the small groups to report out to the large group, giving a recap of the points made in their discussions.

Discussion Questions

- What are your institution's norms in each area? What are your preferences? What are the norms of other cultures?

- In which areas are there the biggest differences in preferences?

- Which differences cause problems, misunderstandings, or obstacles that hinder care, service, and teamwork?

- What adaptations could we make?

Caveats, Considerations, and Adaptations

- It may be difficult for individuals to see the cultural influence behind certain behaviors. You may need to help by giving additional examples or asking participants from other cultures to share examples.

- It is important to avoid giving the impression that people from other cultures are so different and that other norms are so strange that we cannot understand them. One way is to present sets of differences as a continuum, for example, from conformity to individualism. Peer pressure and group solidarity are powerful shapers of behavior in mainstream, individualistic U.S. society. In the same way, in cultures that value conformity, individuals do have their own opinions and may want the freedom to do things their own way.

- It is also important to avoid creating new stereotypes about different cultural groups. It can be insightful to have individuals from the same culture discuss how differently they interpret their own culture's norms. The group can then see that all those of a particular group (African-Americans, Cambodians, Russians, Israelis, and so forth) are not the same and that there are as many differences within a group as from group to group.

- This activity can also be expanded by having the group identify mainstream norms using popular sayings and aphorisms that express cultural values, for example:

  Better late than never, but better never late.

  A penny saved is a penny earned.

  You are your brother's keeper.

  If you don't have anything nice to say, don't say anything at all.

  Don't put off until tomorrow what you could do today.

  Don't be penny wise and pound foolish.

  The squeaky wheel gets the grease.

  The early bird gets the worm.

  Blood is thicker than water.

  If you want something done, give it to a busy person.

🖫 ASPECTS OF CULTURE:
THEIR IMPACT IN A HEALTH CARE SETTING

Directions: The following chart gives you an opportunity to make some notes about cultural differences you have encountered in each of these ten areas of cultural programming. Then make notes about how your institution might meet different preferences and needs and be more welcoming to people of all backgrounds.

Aspects of Culture	Examples of Cultural Differences Among Patients or Staff	Adaptations Required of Health Care Institution
1. **Sense of Self and Space** • Distance • Touch • Formal/Informal • Open/Closed		
2. **Communication and Language** • Language/Dialect • Gestures/ Expressions/Tone • Direct/Indirect		
3. **Dress and Appearance** • Clothing • Hair • Grooming		
4. **Food and Eating Habits** • Food Restrictions/ Taboos • Utensils/Hands • Manners		

Source: Chart adapted with permission from *Managing Diversity: A Complete Desk Reference and Planning Guide.* Lee Gardenswartz and Anita Rowe. Burr Ridge, IL: Irwin Professional, 1993. "Aspects of Culture" adapted from *Managing Cultural Differences,* Second Edition, Philip R. Harris and Robert T. Moran (Gulf Publishing, Houston, 1987).

Aspects of Culture	Examples of Cultural Differences Among Patients or Staff	Adaptations Required of Health Care Institution
5. **Time and Time Consciousness** • Promptness • Age/Status • Pace		
6. **Relationships** • Family • Age/Gender/Kindred • Status		
7. **Values and Norms** • Group vs. Individual • Independence vs. Conformity • Privacy • Respect • Competition vs. Cooperation		
8. **Beliefs and Attitudes** • Religion • Position of Women • Social Order/Authority		
9. **Mental Processes and Learning** • Left/Right Brain Emphasis • Logic/Intuition		
10. **Work Habits and Practices** • Work Ethic • Rewards/Promotions • Status of Type of Work • Division of Labor/Organization		

Directions for Using Expanding Cultural Interpretations

Objectives

- To reduce the risk of misinterpreting behaviors in a diverse environment.

- To make conscious the process of assigning meaning to behavior.

- To increase cross-cultural understanding and improve relationships.

Intended Audience

- Participants in diversity training.

- Staff who serve patients and family members of other cultures.

- Members of diverse teams.

- Managers of diverse work groups.

Time

- 45 minutes.

Materials

- Copies of the Expanding Cultural Interpretations worksheet for each participant.

- Pens or pencils.

Suggested Procedures

- Explain that when dealing with others we follow a three-step process. We observe their behavior, interpret it, then act on our interpretation. However, that interpretation is generally made using our own cultural programming. If the interpretation is inaccurate, our action will probably be ineffective—or even harmful.

- Give a few examples that illustrate the point and solicit examples from the group as well. (Examples can also be found in Chapters 3 and 4 of *Managing Diversity in Health Care.*)

- Ask participants to fill out the worksheet by jotting down their interpretations of the meaning of any of the behaviors listed that would be significant to them.

- Have participants form pairs or threesomes to share their interpretations. Have them suggest additional interpretations of each behavior, based on their knowledge and experience.

- Lead a large group discussion of insights, learnings, and applications.

Discussion Questions

- What meanings do you assign to the behaviors you pay attention to?

- What is the consequence of your interpretation?

- What other meanings of behaviors did you become aware of during this activity?

- How might you respond the next time you encounter a behavior that you previously might have misinterpreted?

Caveats, Considerations, and Adaptations

- Participants may show irritation at having to question their interpretations of behaviors. Help them understand that questioning our interpretations and finding out more about the other person's intended meaning can increase our effectiveness.

- Participants may ask where they can obtain more information about other cultural norms. If so, direct them to some of the culture-specific books listed in Chapter 12 or to the listing of resources in *Managing Diversity in Health Care.*

- If participants have had very little exposure to other cultures, it may be difficult for them to speculate about other meanings of the behaviors. In such a case, you may need to give more examples.

💾 EXPANDING CULTURAL INTERPRETATIONS

Directions: In the middle column, write what each behavior means to you. Then, based on your knowledge of other cultures and your discussions with others, write in the third column what that same behavior might mean to someone of a different culture or background.

Behavior	What It Means to Me	What It Might Mean to the Other Person
Example: Not making eye contact	The individual is sneaky, unassertive, or inattentive.	The individual is showing respect and deference to the speaker.
Not making eye contact		
Saying "yes" or nodding when he/she does not understand		
Giving a soft handshake		
Standing very close when talking		
Spending time in small talk		
Arriving late to an appointment		

Source: Adapted from *The Lending and Diversity Handbook.* © Lee Gardenswartz and Anita Rowe. Burr Ridge, IL: Irwin Professional, 1996. Used with permission.

Behavior	What It Means to Me	What It Might Mean to the Other Person
Bringing family members to an appointment		
Addressing you by Dr./Mr./Mrs./Ms., rather than first name		
Laughing and smiling a lot (when nothing seems funny)		
Arriving without the necessary paperwork		
Not knowing the answers to questions or having needed information		
Avoiding filling out paperwork/forms		
Giving inaccurate information		
Consulting with other family members before making a decision		
Not following a prescribed course of treatment		

Chapter 7

Achieving Practical Cultural Literacy

THIS CHAPTER IS DEVOTED TO HELPING YOU to help participants understand the relationship between ethnic cultural norms and the effective delivery of health care services. The very definition and perception of effective health care is strongly influenced by culture; Chapter 4 in *Managing Diversity in Health Care* clearly demonstrates how. The training activities in this section enable health care practitioners to transition from the conceptual to the concrete. The activities help the trainer to apply differences in viewpoints, attitudes, practices, and beliefs to the implementation of excellent health care treatment for a pluralistic population.

Directions for Using Who's Involved in Making Health Care Decisions?

Objectives

- To increase understanding of the range of preferences regarding involving others in health care decisions.

- To increase sensitivity to others' preferences.

Intended Audience

- Participants in cultural diversity training.

- Managers of direct service staff.

- Staff who serve diverse patients and family members.

Time

- 45 minutes.

Materials

- Copies of the Who's Involved in Making Health Care Decisions? worksheet for each participant.

- Pens or pencils.

Suggested Procedures

- Give a brief explanation of cultural norms influencing health care decision making, based on Chapter 4 of *Managing Diversity in Health Care*.

- Have participants fill out their worksheets, checking who they would involve in each kind of health care decision.

- Place participants in pairs, threesomes, or small groups to share their responses with one another.

- Lead a total group discussion.

Discussion Questions

- What similarities and differences surfaced in your discussion about whom to involve?

- What considerations would influence you to involve others?

- What are the advantages and disadvantages of your preferences?

- Would your preferences change if the decisions were about a loved one rather than about yourself?

- What differences in preferences have you seen in your interactions with patients of various backgrounds?

Caveats, Considerations, and Adaptations

- This activity can be used as a warm-up for a lecturette and discussion about health care decision making. If this option is used, have participants respond to the worksheet individually, then take a quick tally of responses and lead a total group discussion.

- It would be instructive to have data regarding these preferences from various patient groups in your service area. A survey, conducted ahead of time with patients of other cultures, could provide interesting data for comparison with participants' preferences.

- Participants can be asked to think of a patient of another culture whom they have dealt with recently and then also respond to the checklist as though they were that patient, using S for self and P for patient to distinguish responses.

💾 WHO'S INVOLVED IN MAKING HEALTH CARE DECISIONS?

Directions: Consider who you would involve if you had to make any of the health care decisions about those issues listed in the first column. Place a check in the box of any individual or group you would include in your decision making.

Type of Health Care Decision	Me	My Parent(s)	My Spouse	My Child/ Children	My Sibling(s)	Other
Selecting a Provider						
Minor Surgery						
Major Surgery						
Chemotherapy						
Radiation						
Life Support/Do Not Resuscitate						
Blood Transfusion						
Nursing Home Placement						
Dealing with the Results						
Dealing with a Prognosis						
Following a Treatment/ Prescription						

Directions for Using How Culturally Sensitive Are You?

Objectives

- To increase sensitivity about cultural differences in health care norms and practices.

- To stimulate caregivers to learn more about the patients they serve.

Intended Audience

- Medical staff who serve diverse patients.

- Physicians who serve diverse patients.

- Managers of direct care departments.

Time

- 45 minutes.

Materials

- Copies of the How Culturally Sensitive Are You? A Checklist for Care Givers worksheet for all participants.

- Pens or pencils.

Suggested Procedures

- Introduce the topic by asking participants if they have ever been surprised by a cultural difference in a patient's response, reaction, or question. Lead a discussion of the examples that are shared.

- Ask participants to think of a patient from another cultural background and then complete the checklist.

- Have participants share their responses in pairs, threesomes, or small groups.

- Next ask participants to brainstorm a list of ways they can gain more information about these aspects of the patient's preferences, knowledge, beliefs, and backgrounds.

Discussion Questions

- Which aspects of caregiving did you know most about for this patient? How did you gain this knowledge?

- Which aspects do you know least about? How could you have found more of the information you needed?

- What ways have you found effective for persuading patients to disclose critical information?

- What prevents you from obtaining the information you need? How can you overcome these obstacles?

Caveats, Considerations, and Adaptations

- It may be helpful to offer resources that provide culture-specific information to participants. Having reprints of articles and copies of books available at the session or listing those available in your organization's library would be helpful.

💾 HOW CULTURALLY SENSITIVE ARE YOU? A CHECKLIST FOR CARE GIVERS

Directions: Think of a patient you now serve or have served recently who is of another culture. Assess your own cultural sensitivity as a care giver by checking the appropriate response for each statement below.

	Very Much	Somewhat	Very Little
1. I know how this patient defines his/her condition or illness and its cause.			
2. I know how much information he/she wants about the condition.			
3. I know which family members or others the patient wants included in discussions and decisions.			
4. I know the patient's and family's wishes regarding life support.			
5. I know what other treatments and/or practitioners the patient uses.			
6. I know what medications the patient uses.			
7. I know what form of medication the patient prefers.			
8. I know the patient's religious/ethical views regarding health, illness, and death.			
9. I know about the patient's life history (e.g., where born and raised, education, length of time in the U.S.).			
10. I know about the general health beliefs and practices of the patient's culture.			
11. I know how the patient views the body and its functioning.			
12. I know how the patient views my role as well as his/her expectations of me.			

Directions for Scoring

Add the check marks for each column. The more "very much" answers you gave, the more culturally sensitive you are toward patients. After assessing your responses, list two things you could do to be a more responsive caregiver below.

Survey Item	Suggestions
1.	
2.	

Directions for Using Key Cultural Values Impacting Care: My Comfort Zone

Objectives

- To understand one's own cultural comfort and preferences.

- To gain awareness about the impact of culture in the health care environment.

- To increase one's comfort with a variety of norms.

Intended Audience

- All staff who have patient or family contact in a health care environment.

- Managers trying to help staff give culturally appropriate care.

- Trainers who teach cross-cultural norms to respective employees.

Time

- 40 minutes.

Materials

- Copies of the Key Cultural Values Impacting Care: My Comfort Zone worksheet for all participants.

- Copies of An Overall Glance at Key Cultural Values and How They Impact Care for all participants (to be distributed at the end of the learning activity).

- Pens or pencils.

- An easel, newsprint pad, and felt-tipped markers (optional).

- Felt-tipped markers for each person are helpful for this activity if done in pairs. Make sure that the participants in each pair have different colors of markers.

Suggested Procedures

- Begin by asking participants what cultural norms among the various patient populations have been hard to adapt to. You may choose to chart their responses or just listen to the information and engage in a discussion about the "whys" of the discomfort and the adaptations they have made.

- Give a brief explanation about each of the five cultural norms on the Key Cultural Values Impacting Care worksheet (see Chapter 4 in *Managing Diversity in Health Care*) and distribute the worksheet to everyone.

- Have each participant put an "X" to indicate his or her comfort zone or preference in each of the five areas.

- Ask participants to take a pencil or marker and connect the X's to make an individual profile.

- Put participants into pairs or small groups and ask them to compare profiles, focusing on their current profile, what this profile might suggest, where they need to increase their comfort levels, and how they might do so.

- Ask everyone to share their results in the total group, which is useful for increasing group cohesion and interpersonal understanding.

Discussion Questions

- Look at your existing profile. Draw parentheses around the X's that indicate your comfort zone. When you look at your expanded profile, what does this information suggest to you?

- Where do you most need to expand your comfort zone, given your patient population?

- How might you do this?

- What are the consequences of doing nothing differently?

Caveats, Considerations, and Adaptations

- This worksheet can also be used as a team exercise. First, draw the worksheet as large as possible on the newsprint pad. Then have each team member use a different color marker to draw his or her profile. Finally, have the team look at what they need to improve as a group to serve their patients and families. This team information can also be applied to serving internal customers as well.

🖫 KEY CULTURAL VALUES IMPACTING CARE: MY COMFORT ZONE

Directions: On the continua below, place an X indicating where you are most comfortable. Connect the dots to make a profile.

STATUS

Inherited .... Earned

PRIVACY

Closed .... Open

FATALISM

External locus .... Internal locus
of control   of control

INDIVIDUAL/GROUP

Individual .... Group

RIGHT TO KNOW

Information .... Information
withheld   shared

AN OVERALL GLANCE AT KEY CULTURAL VALUES AND HOW THEY IMPACT CARE			
Value	**Tendencies in the Mainstream U.S.**	**Tendencies in Other Cultures**	**Implications for Health Care Provider**
Status	Earned through accomplishments; status given to celebrity, certain diplomas, titles, etc., but rarely inherited through family, gender, or age.	Position in family, title, gender, family heritage, and age, are all given status.	How decisions are made about treatment and who is involved in decisions is impacted by status. In cultures in which status is inherited by things such as gender, age, and title, the positions must be acknowledged in order to build relationships and trust.
Privacy	As a whole, society is more open in talking about psychological and physiological conditions; even talk shows and newspapers are vehicles for carrying information.	Respecting privacy and keeping personal matters within the family is a top priority; modesty and shame, particularly for women, also ties in to this concept.	A value on privacy may make it harder to obtain necessary information. Relationship building is key, and gaining insight from cultural interpreters can be helpful.
Fatalism	Internal locus of control is dominant in U.S. There is a strong sense of control and shaping one's own destiny and accepting responsibility for one's physical health.	External locus of control is more important in many other cultures. Sense of fatalism and predestination can be impacted by education, socioeconomics, and acculturation. God's will may influence health or illness.	For people who are strong fatalists, the idea that a disease or condition is meant to be, or is God's will, may impact attitude toward treatment and prevent intervening on one's own behalf. You may need to consider the value of prayer and the assistance of a spiritual leader.
Individual/ Group	Although there is a strong emphasis on teamness today, there is a deeply ingrained emphasis on the individual, particularly as it relates to reward structures.	In most cultures in the world, individual will, need, and desire is sublimated to the group. The welfare of the family or group is seen as paramount.	You may need bigger waiting rooms for extended families; decisions may be made by a large group; the patient cannot be considered in isolation.
Right to Know	The right to know is strong; the sense that information is power works well in the U.S.; although some people clearly favor denial and lack of information, most want the straight scoop.	Full information is not wanted and can negatively impact patient's psychological well-being. Stigma and shame are attached to some illnesses.	There is a critical need to learn about the patient. Get clues from family and patient before telling all. Must take into account perceptions about the illness and the stigma or shame attached. It is often desirable to withhold information from the patient, particularly when there is a terminal diagnosis.

Chapter 8

Improving Communication in Diverse Environments

SOME OF THE MOST FREQUENTLY REPORTED DIFFICULTIES in diverse settings are those centering around obstacles to communication. Both language and cultural differences can be sources of misunderstanding, misinterpretation, and perceived slights. Because so much of health care depends on getting and giving clear, accurate information and on establishing trusting relationships, effective cross-cultural communication is critical. The following activities help participants develop competence in communicating with staff and patients of different backgrounds.

Content information that supports these activities can be found in Chapter 5 in *Managing Diversity in Health Care*.

Directions for Using Language and You

Objectives

- To initiate discussion about language differences on the job.

- To identify specific issues and obstacles to cross-cultural communication.

Intended Audience

- Staff working with physicians, patients, and families in multilingual environments.

- Managers of culturally diverse teams.

- Staff working on culturally diverse teams.

Time

- 30 minutes.

Materials

- Copies of Language and You for all participants.

- Pens or pencils.

Suggested Procedures

- Have participants take a few minutes to write completions for the open-ended statements on the worksheet; then have them pair up and take turns sharing their responses to each question.

- Lead a total group discussion of the issues that surfaced.

Discussion Questions

- What insights did you have as you shared responses?

- What are the most difficult aspects involved in intercultural communication?

- What factors help communication in multilingual settings? What factors hinder it?

- What have you done that helps?

- What more could you do?

Caveats, Considerations, and Adaptations

- To shorten the activity each participant can select only two or three of the statements to complete and share.

- One or two of these open-ended statements can be used as a warm-up for a meeting or discussion of cross-cultural communication obstacles. In such a setting, participants would take turns completing one or two pre-selected statements.

🖫 **LANGUAGE AND YOU**

Directions: Complete the following open-ended statements about use of language on the job. Then pair up with a co-worker to share your responses.

- When I hear someone speaking with an accent, I …

  _____

  _____

- I'm considered by others to have an accent when …

  _____

  _____

- When others speak a language I don't understand in my presence, I …

  _____

  _____

- Learning another language is …

  _____

  _____

- When I speak another language, I …

  _____

  _____

- I speak my native language at work because …

  _____

  _____

- I get most frustrated with language barriers when …

  _____

  _____

- When there's a language barrier, I wish others would …

  _____

  _____

- I wish I could speak another language when …

  _____

  _____

- I've been most successful in overcoming language barriers by …

  _____

- Cross-cultural communication can be improved when …

  _____

  _____

Directions for Using Intercultural Hooks That Block Communication

Objectives

- To identify personal cross-cultural "hooks."

- To recognize the cultural sources of irritating behaviors.

- To overcome culturally rooted blocks to productive relationships.

Intended Audience

- Participants in diversity training focusing on cross-cultural communication.

- Managers of diverse teams.

- Employees who serve patients and/or work with colleagues of other cultures.

Time

- 30 minutes.

Materials

- Copies of Intercultural Hooks That Block Communication for all participants.

- Pens or pencils.

Suggested Procedures

- Introduce the activity by explaining that communication involves an affective component and that there is generally an important emotional aspect operating in cross-cultural communication. Give an example or two. (See Chapter 5 in *Managing Diversity in Health Care.*)

- Tell participants to check those behaviors on the worksheet that they find irritating, then to jot down their typical reaction to each behavior they check.

- Have participants form pairs or small groups and share responses, then try to determine the dimensions of culture that may be at the source of each behavior checked.

- Lead a large group discussion of insights, new perspectives gained, and applications.

Discussion Questions

- What are your typical reactions when you get "hooked"?

- How does this affect how you deal with the situation?

- What have you done to overcome this block?

- Which areas of cultural programming come into play in those hooks you checked?

- How have you been able to adapt to a particular norm that you find irritating?

- What can you do to help others to adapt to a particular norm that irritates them?

Caveats, Considerations, and Adaptations

- This activity must be coupled with an explanation of cultural factors that influence communication. It can be used as a lead-in to the topic or as a follow-up activity to deepen understanding and stimulate application.

- Participants may find some behaviors unacceptable and may be unwilling to get beyond their emotional reactions. In cases such as this, help the participant focus on effectiveness by asking questions such as:

    How is this reaction working for you?

    What do you want to achieve in this situation?

    What is the best way to achieve your objective?

⬛ INTERCULTURAL HOOKS THAT BLOCK COMMUNICATION

Directions: Put a check mark next to any of the cross-cultural "hooks" that could result in frustration or negative interactions between you and a patient, family member, physician, or co-worker. Then, as you read each item, jot down your typical reaction to that behavior.

❑ Nodding or saying "yes" even though not understanding.

❑ Speaking in a language other than English.

❑ Deferring to others when asked a question.

❑ Speaking loudly.

❑ Lacking nonverbal feedback (e.g., facial expression, nodding).

❑ Speaking softly.

❑ Avoiding eye contact.

❑ Smiling and laughing when nothing is humorous.

❑ Giving a soft, limp handshake.

❑ Standing very close when talking.

❑ Speaking with a heavy accent or limited English.

❑ Making small talk and not getting to the point.

❑ Not providing necessary information.

❑ Not taking initiative to ask questions.

❑ Calling/not calling you by your first name.

❑ Discounting, avoiding, or refusing to deal with you because of gender.

❑ Speaking in a high pitched voice.

❑ Asking personal questions.

❑ Using formal titles in addressing people.

❑ Other _____

❑ Other _____

Directions for Using Cultural Differences Affecting Communication with Patients and Staff

Objectives

- To increase understanding about cultural differences influencing communication.

- To raise awareness about the underlying causes of some communication difficulties.

- To encourage greater tolerance for cultural differences.

- To encourage flexibility in communicating with others of different cultural backgrounds.

Intended Audience

- Participants in a diversity skills training session.

- Employees working on diverse teams or serving diverse patients and family members.

- Managers of diverse work groups.

Time

- 45 minutes.

Materials

- Copies of the Cultural Differences Affecting Communication with Patients and Staff worksheet for all participants.

- Pens or pencils.

- Easel and newsprint pad (optional).

- Enough felt-tipped markers so that each participant has two different colored markers.

Suggested Procedures

- Ask participants to think of a recent incident when cross-cultural communication was difficult. Ask them to consider what aspect of the other person's communication made it seem difficult.

- Explain that both culture and personality influence an individual's communication style and say that the next activity will give them a greater understanding of these variables.

- Give a brief lecturette about cultural variables influencing communication. (See Chapter 5 in *Managing Diversity in Health Care.*)

- Explain the objective of the activity, distribute worksheets, and give directions.

- Tell participants to mark, with an X, the spot on each continuum that represents their own preferences and behavior as communicators. Then have them connect their X's with a colored marker to obtain their individual profiles.

- Now ask them to think about a co-worker, patient, or physician from another culture and to place a large check mark on each continuum representing how the other person communicates. Using a different color marker, they should connect the check marks to make a profile of this individual's communication style.

- Tell participants to pair up and discuss these two profiles and the effects they have on communication between the two people.

- Lead a total group discussion of insights and applications.

- Ask participants to share with their partners one action they could take to overcome one of the communication blocks they profiled.

Discussion Quest\ions

- What does your profile say about you as a communicator?

- What are the biggest differences between the two profiles on the worksheet?

- What differences are hardest for you to deal with? How can you help yourself communicate better with those who have these preferences and behaviors?

- Which of your preferences and behaviors might be difficult for others to deal with?

- What can you do to improve communication with those who have a different profile from you?

- How are you willing to adapt or modify your preferences and behaviors?

- How can you help the other person adapt or modify his or her style, assuming there is a willingness to do so?

Caveats, Considerations, and Adaptations

- This activity can be done as part of team building for a multicultural work group that is having communication difficulties. Team members can share their profiles and receive feedback from one another.

- The team can also draw a composite profile on a poster-sized enlargement of the sheet, with each team member drawing his or her profile using a different colored marker or symbol. Differences can then be pointed out and discussed.

- In still another variation, individual profiles on worksheets can be posted on the walls and left for team members to see at the breaks throughout the workshop.

▣ CULTURAL DIFFERENCES AFFECTING COMMUNICATION WITH PATIENTS AND STAFF

Directions: Place an X on each continuum showing your preferences. Then place a ✓ to show the preferences and norms of one of your patients or co-workers of a different cultural background.

Language:
English only .... Other language(s)

Directness:
Direct .... Indirect

Gestures:
Little body movement .... Much body movement
and facial expression   and facial expression

Distance:
Distant, arm's length .... Close, nose to nose

Touch:
No touching .... Touching

Topics:
Impersonal .... Personal

Formality:
Formal/structured .... Informal/casual

Address:
Surnames, titles .... First names

Relationship/Task Balance:
Emphasis on .... Emphasis on task
Relationship   accomplishment

Status:
Hierarchical .... Egalitarian

Pace:
Brisk, fast pace .... Measured, slow pace

Pitch:
High .... Low

Source: Adapted from *The Lending and Diversity Handbook.* © Lee Gardenswartz and Anita Rowe. Burr Ridge, IL: Irwin Professional, 1996. Used with permission.

Directions for Using Giving Directions and Explanations in Culturally Sensitive Ways

Objectives

- To practice four techniques useful in intercultural communication.
- To learn communication methods that can lower the risk of loss of face to either party.

Intended Audience

- Participants in a diversity skill-building training session focusing on communication.
- Employees working on multicultural teams or serving patients and family members of other cultures.
- Managers of multicultural work groups who need to give feedback to members of the group.

Time

- 45 minutes.

Materials

- Copies of the Giving Directions and Explanations in Culturally Sensitive Ways worksheet for all participants.
- Pens or pencils.

Suggested Procedures

- Give a brief lecturette about cultural factors influencing the process of giving directions, explanations, and feedback; then explain four techniques for doing so in culturally sensitive ways. (See Chapter 5 in *Managing Diversity in Health Care*.)
- Explain the objectives of the activity, distribute the worksheets, and give directions. If necessary, lead the total group in one or two examples from the left-hand column first, explaining why it would be less effective. (See Chapter 5 in *Managing Diversity in Health Care*.)
- Give participants time to write their statements on the worksheets using the four methods described.
- Have participants form small groups (three or four people) to share their statements, checking one another to be sure each technique is appropriately used.

- Tell groups to share examples of their statements with the large group.

- Lead a total group discussion of reactions, learnings, and applications.

- Using the techniques learned, have participants individually write one explanation, direction, or feedback statement they can actually use with someone in their own work situations.

Discussion Questions

- What were your reactions to trying these techniques?

- What was easy? Difficult?

- Where could you use these methods to increase the effectiveness of your communication?

Caveats, Considerations, and Adaptations

- Participants may balk at using techniques that feel unnatural or artificial. Explain that these are not intended to replace their customary communication methods, but to augment them, giving more options to use. Also emphasize that techniques become more natural with practice and use.

- In order to make the practice more true to life, create different "bad example" statements or elicit examples from the group.

- Participants may resist using passive language and impersonal statements, feeling that doing so is "beating around the bush." It is important to explain the cultural differences between more direct, content-oriented communication (the mainstream U.S. norm) and more indirect, context-oriented communication (the norm in the Arab world and much of Asia). (See Chapter 5, pages 103–104, and Chapter 4, pages 44–46.) As you explain, be sure to give actual examples that clearly illustrate the differences in a health care environment.

🖫 GIVING DIRECTIONS AND EXPLANATIONS IN CULTURALLY SENSITIVE WAYS

Directions: When you give directions or explanations in multicultural situations, there is a potential for misunderstandings and misinterpretations that can lead to loss of face. This worksheet gives you a chance to practice four communication techniques that can lower this risk and help your message be effectively received and understood. In each section, follow the suggested technique and change the ineffective statement in the left-hand column to a more effective one on the right.

1. Make observations about *behaviors* and/or *situations* rather than *judgments* or *evaluations*.

Judgment/Evaluation	Behavior/Situation
a. This form is incomplete.	*We need the name of your insurance company and your member number on page 2.*
b. This application is fraudulent.	
c. Your health history information is inadequate.	

2. Be less direct by using the passive voice. Make the object the subject.

Active	Passive
a. You've made too many mistakes on this form.	*There are some errors on page 2 of this form.*
b. You're late with this information. I needed it last week.	
c. What was the name of the medication you took before?	

3. Be less direct by making comments Impersonal. Omit the "you."

Personal	Impersonal
a. You forgot to get the signature of your spouse.	*The signature of your spouse needs to be here.*
b. You didn't attach copies of the required documents to your application.	
c. You can't expect me to understand these documents in another language.	

4. Be positive. Tell what you do want, not what you do not want.

Negative	Positive
a. Don't leave carts in the doorway.	*Move carts to the side of the doorway while serving patients.*
b. Don't allow children to play with the brochures.	
c. Don't bring this back without the necessary documents.	

Source: Adapted from *The Lending and Diversity Handbook.* © Lee Gardenswartz and Anita Rowe. Burr Ridge, IL: Irwin Professional, 1996. Used with permission.

Directions for Using Communicating Across Language Barriers

Objectives

- To gain techniques to increase effectiveness in communicating across language barriers.

- To assess oneself as a communicator in intercultural situations.

Intended Audience

- Participants in a diversity skills training session focusing on communication.

- Employees who work with or serve limited-English-speaking individuals.

- Managers of limited-English-speaking individuals.

- Volunteers who work in multilingual settings.

Time

- 45 minutes.

Materials

- Copies of the Communicating Across Language Barriers worksheet for all participants.

- Easel with newsprint pad.

- Felt-tipped markers.

- Pens or pencils.

Suggested Procedures

- Introduce the topic by asking participants one or both of the following questions:

  What different languages do you deal with daily?

  What is the most difficult part of communicating with individuals who do not speak your language(s)?

- Ask participants to brainstorm techniques they have used that facilitate communication in these situations and chart their responses.

- Next ask the group to brainstorm techniques that do not work and chart their responses.

- State the objectives of the activity, distribute the worksheet, and give directions. Briefly explain each technique. (See Chapter 5 in *Managing Diversity in Health Care.*)

- Tell participants to respond to the worksheet, assessing their own use of the ten techniques for communicating across language barriers.

- Have participants share their responses in pairs or small groups, discussing what they could do more of to improve communication with limited English-speaking individuals.

- Lead a total group discussion of applications.

Discussion Questions

- Which of these techniques have you not generally used?

- What obstacles have prevented you from using them? What could you do to overcome these obstacles?

- What other techniques have you found helpful?

- What could you do to enhance your effectiveness in communicating across language barriers?

- What one new technique will you be willing to try in the next week? How will you measure its effectiveness?

Caveats, Considerations, and Adaptations

- If time is short, this activity can be processed in the large group while you lead a total group discussion.

- Participants may show irritation at having to learn ways to communicate with limited English speakers, insisting that others should learn English. It is important to help participants see how communicating effectively with limited English-speaking individuals is to their own benefit. Ask questions such as:

  What will happen if you don't communicate effectively with others who speak limited English?

  How will your job be easier if you do communicate well?

  What is your main objective during these interactions?

  What is the most effective way to achieve this objective?

💾 **COMMUNICATING ACROSS LANGUAGE BARRIERS**

Directions: Check off each of the following behaviors you usually use when communicating with someone who is a limited speaker of your language.

_____ 1. I make it visual, using pictures, signs, diagrams, and other visual symbols.

_____ 2. I demonstrate as I explain and, when possible, I have the individual perform the task as I watch.

_____ 3. I use the other person's language, either in writing or speaking.

_____ 4. I speak slowly, pausing between sentences.

_____ 5. I use simple vocabulary and avoid using idiomatic expressions such as "It's a slam dunk," or "What's the bottom line?"

_____ 6. I repeat, using different words. If possible, I try to use words that are more internationally known, for example, *problem* rather than *dilemma, glitch,* or *snafu, operation* rather than *surgical procedure.*

_____ 7. I expect confusion, avoid asking people if they understand, and do not take a nodding head, smile, or "yes" to mean I have been understood.

_____ 8. I obtain the help of an interpreter when I need it.

_____ 9. I try to walk in the other person's shoes, imagining how this difficulty might feel.

_____ 10. I smile, showing warmth and friendliness, but I do not laugh.

Source: Adapted from *The Diversity Tool Kit.* © Lee Gardenswartz and Anita Rowe. Burr Ridge, IL: Irwin Professional, 1994. Used with permission.

Directions for Using Guidelines for Using Interpreters

Objectives

- To increase skills in using interpreters.

- To assess one's effectiveness in using interpreters.

- To identify additional approaches to improving communication with the aid of an interpreter.

Intended Audience

- Staff who need to make use of interpreters in communicating with other staff, patients, or the public.

- Managers who make use of interpreters.

- Participants in cross-cultural communication training.

Time

- 45 minutes.

Materials

- Copies of Guidelines for Using Interpreters for all participants.

- Pens or pencils.

- An easel and newsprint paper.

- Masking tape.

- Felt-tipped markers.

Suggested Procedures

- Ask how many individuals have made use of interpreters and then ask a few who have to volunteer to describe their experiences.

- Ask participants to fill out the checklist.

- Explain that, in general, the more items on which they responded "usually," the more effectively they are using interpreters.

- Lead a discussion of any of the suggestions that there are questions about or that surprised participants. (See Chapter 5 in *Managing Diversity in Health Care*.)

- Have participants form small groups and share those guidelines that they seldom follow. Have each group select and focus on one or two seldom-followed guidelines, and then brainstorm obstacles they face in following them, list them on the newsprint, and tape them to the wall.

- Next have the groups think of ways to overcome these obstacles in order to make better use of each guideline. For example, an obstacle to utilizing professional interpreters may be that there are none employed by the hospital. Actions they could take might include utilizing AT&T's language hot line; training and certifying bilingual staff to serve as interpreters; or suggesting to management that interpreters be hired for the most needed languages.

- Tell each group to report its results to the total group, using its newsprint sheet as a visual aid.

Discussion Questions
- Which guidelines do you generally follow?

- Which were a surprise to you?

- Which do you have questions about?

- What keeps you from following those you marked as rarely used?

- What actions can you take or would you suggest your organization take to make better use of interpreters?

- What is one thing you will do differently the next time you communicate with the help of an interpreter?

Caveats, Considerations, and Adaptations
- Following some of the guidelines may be out of the sphere of control of the staff members. In these cases, help them identify who in the organization they need to involve in order to get help.

🖫 GUIDELINES FOR USING INTERPRETERS

Directions: Think of a few times recently when you have used an interpreter. Then respond to the items on the checklist below based on your behavior.

	Usually	Sometimes	Rarely
1. I use a professionally trained interpreter.			
2. I use an interpreter who is older than the patient.			
3. I use an interpreter of the same gender as the patient.			
4. I use an interpreter from a similar socio-political background as the patient.			
5. I introduce the interpreter formally at the beginning of the conversation, interview, or session.			
6. I address and face the patient, not the interpreter.			
7. I meet the interpreter ahead of time and explain the case and my objectives in the interaction.			
8. I speak clearly, simply, and slowly, pausing to give the interpreter time to relay the information.			

Source: Adapted from Nikki L. Katalanos, "When Yes Means No: Verbal and Non-Verbal Communication of Southeast Asian Refugees in the New Mexico Health Care System." Unpublished master's thesis.

Directions for Using Practice in Conducting Culturally Sensitive Medical Interviews: Using the LEARN Steps

Objectives

- To increase skills and effectiveness in conducting medical interviews with patients of other cultures.

- To practice applying the LEARN steps in interviewing patients.

Intended Audience

- Staff and physicians who conduct medical interviews with patients.

- Managers of staff who conduct medical interviews.

- Participants in cross-cultural communication training.

Time

- 45 minutes.

Materials

- Copies of the Practice in Conducting Culturally Sensitive Medical Interviews: Using the LEARN Steps worksheet for each participant.

- Pens or pencils.

- Prepared, printed case examples (optional).

Suggested Procedures

- Introduce the topic by giving a few examples of cultural differences that impact and impair communication in medical interviews. (See Chapter 5 in *Managing Diversity in Health Care.*)

- Give a brief lecturette on the LEARN steps, giving examples of questions and statements at each step. (See Chapter 5.)

- Following the lecturette, direct participants to group into threesomes to practice in a role-play format. In each threesome, assign one participant the role of patient, a second the role of the staff member, and the third as an observer. The "patient" can either create a situation, identity, and illness based on his or her experience with a patient from another culture or can use a written description of his or her identity and situation you have prepared in advance. The "staff member" conducts a medical interview with the "patient" utilizing the LEARN steps. The "observer" watches the interaction and makes notes on the worksheet about the "staff member's" behaviors and actions in using the LEARN steps. At the end of a 7 to 8 minute "interview," the "observer" gives the "staff member" feedback, sharing the observations made. "Staff member" and "patient" then share their reactions. This process is repeated two more times so that each person has a chance to play all three roles.

- Lead a total group debriefing of the practice role plays using the discussion questions below.

Discussion Questions

- What did you do best during your interview?

- What LEARN steps were easiest to use? Most difficult?

- What would you need to do to get better at the steps?

- What did you learn about your own cross-cultural communication?

- What will you do to increase the effectiveness of your next medical interview?

Caveats, Considerations, and Adaptations

- Participants may initially resist participating in a role play. Explain that this activity gives them a chance to practice a different approach in a low-risk setting that allows feedback and learning.

- Participants may have difficulty in coming up with relevant scenarios for the patient role; therefore, preparing written cases that are typical of the kinds of situations encountered by the patient population can be helpful.

- Demonstrating the technique by role playing a scenario in front of the group can be helpful in situations in which role play is difficult for participants.

💾 PRACTICE IN CONDUCTING CULTURALLY SENSITIVE MEDICAL INTERVIEWS: USING THE LEARN STEPS

Directions: Use the worksheet to guide your observation of how the staff member uses the LEARN steps. Under each behavior, make notes about the actions that the staff member took that demonstrated that behavior. For example, the staff member may have encouraged the patient to explain the condition by smiling, asking open-ended questions, and not interrupting. Or the staff member may have verified the patient's understanding by asking the patient to describe how he or she would take the medication.

Step	Observer Notes
	Examples of staff member behavior and actions
L Listen with sympathy and understanding as you elicit information	• Encouraged the patient to explain the condition. • Made the patient feel comfortable. • Solicited more information. • Demonstrated nonjudgmental openness.
E Explain your perception of the problem	• Adjusted the explanation and vocabulary to suit the patient. • Held the patient's attention and interest. • Made use of the patient's values, beliefs, and concepts to explain the problem.

Source: Adapted from Elois Ann Berlin and William C. Fowkes, Jr., "A Teaching Framework for Cross-Cultural Health Care," *The Western Journal of Medicine,* December 1983, *139b,* p. 934.

Step	Observer Notes
	Examples of staff member behavior and actions
A **Acknowledge** differences and similarities	• Pointed out areas of agreement and areas of difference. • Verified the patient's understanding.
R **Recommend** treatment	• Solicited the patient's input about treatment preferences. • Suited the treatment to the patient's lifestyle and preferences.
N **Negotiate** treatment	• Elicited the patient's reaction to the treatment plan. • Adjusted the plan to overcome any obstacles.

Chapter 9

Removing Stereotypes That Block High-Quality Care

TO BE HUMAN IS TO ENGAGE IN BEHAVIORS that label, limit, and stereotype other human beings, either as individuals or as part of a collective identity. This chapter provides activities to assist the trainer in helping participants come to terms with the assumptions they make about others and with how these perceptions or expectations can influence health care delivery and treatment, usually in a way that diminishes it. Working through the learning activities in this chapter will help the health care practitioner acknowledge, come to terms with, and hopefully lessen the use of stereotyping toward other human beings. To further enhance your content knowledge about stereotypes and assumptions, see Chapter 6 in *Managing Diversity in Health Care*.

Directions for Using Assumptions:
What You See Is What You Get

Objectives

- To identify one's own assumptions about others.

- To realize that assumptions often operate at an unconscious level.

- To understand how limiting and inaccurate assumptions can be.

- To develop a mechanism for making participants more conscious of their assumptions.

Intended Audience
- Staff who work directly with patients (especially employees in admitting, at the reception desk, or in patient care).
- Human resources staff.
- Managers of direct patient contact staff.

Time
- 30 to 45 minutes.

Materials
- Copies of Assumptions: What You See Is What You Get worksheets for all participants.
- Pens or pencils.
- Easel and newsprint sheets.
- Felt-tipped markers.

Suggested Procedures
- Introduce the topic with a brief example or discussion of assumptions and how limiting they can be.
- Distribute the worksheet and explain the directions and the objectives of the activity. Ask each participant to write a response to each of the scenarios.
- Put people into pairs or small groups and ask them to discuss their responses, indicating experiences they may have had that made them form these assumptions.
- Pay particular attention to the similarities and differences in responses and use this data for a large group discussion.

Discussion Questions
- What was your reaction to doing this activity when you started writing down your assumptions?
- Which situations generated easy, quick responses? Which were more difficult? If you had trouble coming up with an assumption, can you identify the reason?
- Can you determine why you hold the assumptions you do?
- Did other participants have assumptions that surprised you?
- What impact do these assumptions have on your behavior at work?

- Identify one or two that you will pay particular attention to in the future.

- What will you do to help yourself become more aware of your assumptions? What will you do to minimize this type of thinking?

Caveats, Considerations, and Adaptations

- Tell participants before they begin writing that they will share their responses with others.

- Don't be surprised by nervous laughter, resistance, or some tension. These feelings are a healthy part of the discussion when processing the activity.

- Help participants understand that although some of their assumptions are embarrassing, due to the limits they place on others, it is human to make some assumptions about others. Such an awareness can help employees engage in less limited thinking.

- Have participants go back to their original pair or small group and make a verbal commitment to their growth in this area as a closure.

🖫 ASSUMPTIONS: WHAT YOU SEE IS WHAT YOU GET

Directions: In the right-hand column, jot down what you might assume about an individual described in the left-hand column.

I see . . .	I assume . . .
Someone poorly dressed.	
A patient having a difficult time filling out a form.	
Someone who speaks with a heavy accent.	
A woman with several children.	
Someone speaking another language.	
Someone in a work uniform (e.g., uniform of a mechanic, repair person, mail carrier, or hospital employee).	
A patient who brings no insurance form or other pertinent information.	
A patient who arrives late to an appointment.	
A male patient who appears to be under twenty-five with an earring.	
A large family group who come in together.	
A female patient who appears to be over sixty whose husband answers all the questions.	
Someone with a disheveled, sloppy appearance and poor grooming (dirty hair, nails, or clothing).	
Someone who uses poor grammar.	
Someone who is unable to describe physical symptoms clearly.	
Someone who is modest and/or timid.	
A patient who is intimidated by or deferential to physicians.	

Directions for Using Recognizing Stereotypes

Objectives

- To identify one's own attitudes, biases, and assumptions about certain groups.

- To understand how pervasively the stereotypes are created and reinforced in our culture.

- To refute stereotypes by identifying individuals who disprove the generalization.

Intended Audience

- Employees with responsibility for dealing with patients and their families.

- Human resource staff or trainers whose task is to teach health care employees.

- All employees in the organization or team.

Time

- 45 to 60 minutes.

Materials

- Copies of the Recognizing Stereotypes worksheet for all participants.

- Pens or pencils.

- Easel and newsprint paper.

- Masking tape.

Suggested Procedures

- Begin with an introduction and discussion about stereotypes and assumptions in general. You may wish to try a group brainstorming session in which participants first write down their own stereotypes, or ones they've heard (even if they don't believe them), about physicians, nurses, and health care workers in the United States. Once they make their own lists (2 minutes is all they need), have everyone contribute items from their lists while you chart them in front of the group. Make some brief comments about the nature of stereotyping as a human phenomenon and the negative impacts that result when we do it.

- Hand out the Recognizing Stereotypes worksheet and ask each individual to read the directions and fill it out individually.

- Next have participants pair up with someone they trust and discuss their responses, paying particular attention to the groups they've identified and how much of what they listed can be disproved.

- Hold a large group discussion, ultimately focusing on implications at work in the clinic, hospital, or medical center.

- End with participants going back to their original discussion partners to make a commitment for one change they can make that will minimize the harmful effects of stereotypes.

Discussion Questions

- Which items were difficult to answer? Are there items for which you had no responses? If so, which ones?

- About what groups do you hold negative stereotypes? List as many for each category as come to mind.

- How do these stereotypes shape your interactions at work?

- What is the consequence of continuing to view people as labels or parts of a group, rather than as individuals?

- What can you do to lessen the negative impact of these stereotypes?

Caveats, Considerations, and Adaptations

- Tell participants at the beginning that they will share their responses with others.

- Expect tension and discomfort. The topic of stereotypes often generates discomfort because most of us aren't pleased that we label or limit people. Help participants understand that acknowledgment is the beginning of change.

- Keep people in work teams or larger work groups, rather than pairing them up, and they can chart their responses at stations around the room. This will give you a broader perspective, but some people may be too intimidated to talk about a potentially volatile subject in a small group.

- Do an item analysis and have participants talk about those that were most obvious and easy to answer.

- Depending on how much time you have for discussion, you may want to go directly to those items on the list that are most relevant for how employees view their own patient population.

- Be careful to state clearly that neither you nor anyone in the organization is labeling any group. Rather, you are trying to assess the power of stereotypes and minimize their harmfulness.

💾 RECOGNIZING STEREOTYPES

Directions: Check any of the following assumptions you have *heard* or *held*. Then write the group(s) about which it is said. Finally, in the far right-hand column, write the name of an individual who disproves this stereotype.

		Group	Individual Who Disproves
_____ 1.	Are indigent and can't afford care.	_____	_____
_____ 2.	Are a health risk to the health practitioner.	_____	_____
_____ 3.	Are ignorant and uneducated.	_____	_____
_____ 4.	Do not accept responsibility for their own health.	_____	_____
_____ 5.	Are stable and reliable.	_____	_____
_____ 6.	Are rude and ill-mannered.	_____	_____
_____ 7.	Do not make independent decisions about treatment.	_____	_____
_____ 8.	Are passive and uninvolved in their own care.	_____	_____
_____ 9.	Are pushy and aggressive.	_____	_____
_____ 10.	Do not follow treatment plans (e.g., diet, medication, etc.).	_____	_____
_____ 11.	Drink too much and cause their own problems.	_____	_____
_____ 12.	Have illegitimate children.	_____	_____
_____ 13.	Put a high value on education.	_____	_____
_____ 14.	Are substance abusers.	_____	_____
_____ 15.	Live together in multifamily groups.	_____	_____
_____ 16.	Are clannish and help only their own.	_____	_____
_____ 17.	Lie and cheat to get what they want.	_____	_____
_____ 18.	Do not have medical insurance.	_____	_____
_____ 19.	Do not speak English.	_____	_____
_____ 20.	Are dirty and have lice.	_____	_____

Directions for Using Subjective Factors Influencing Care

Objectives

- To identify one's responses to various patient factors and assess the impact these responses have on the level of care given.

- To understand the role that unconscious assumptions may have on interactions with patients and family members.

- To recognize parts of one's own cultural programming that influence interactions with patients.

Intended Audience

- Nurses, physicians, lab technicians, or any health care employee who has a high level of patient interactions with diverse populations.

- Trainers in the health care field who have a diverse population.

- Managers who lead diverse groups.

Time

- 30 minutes.

Materials

- Copies of Subjective Factors Influencing Care worksheets for all participants.

- Pens or pencils.

Suggested Procedures

- Distribute the questionnaire and explain that patient/employee relationships are a result of the teachings, values, and norms each person brings to every interaction. Because the dynamics and quality of the relationship are dependent on the various interactions, the employee needs to look at: (1) assessments he or she has made about the patient or family member based on some observable factors and (2) the employee's own life experiences and outlook.

- Ask participants to fill out the worksheet according to the directions, checking the appropriate boxes.

- Have participants pair up and discuss the subjective factors that influence patient care.

- Lead a general discussion of what they have learned.

Discussion Questions

- What patient characteristics or behaviors matter most to you?

- What assumptions are you making about others?

- Have you ever found any of your assumptions to be invalid? If so, which ones and when?

- How have your assumptions influenced the quality of your interactions with any patient or his or her family?

- When you look at the reasons why certain factors influence your feelings, which would you say matter the most to you?

- Based on your discussion with your partner, what do you need to do differently?

Caveats, Considerations, and Adaptations

- Introductory comments are critically important. Put them in the context of human behavior so people won't feel defensive. Acknowledge that all human beings make assumptions and that our behaviors and relationships are influenced by these assumptions.

- Set it up as one way to identify concrete factors, which, if better understood, could improve relationships.

- This activity could be done solely as an individual learning experience. In this way, shame or embarrassment would be minimized, but so would learning. By creating safe pairs or small groups and letting people talk honestly, learning is maximized.

💾 SUBJECTIVE FACTORS INFLUENCING CARE

Directions: Check any of these factors that influence your assessment of a patient or family member. As you fill in the boxes, think about how these factors influence the care you give.

Patient's:

☐ Grooming	☐ Eye contact
☐ Dress	☐ Tone of voice
☐ Appearance	☐ Personality
☐ Manners	☐ Interpersonal skills
☐ Promptness	☐ Handshake
☐ Speaking style	☐ Facial expression
☐ Accent	☐ Educational level
☐ Other _____	☐ Body odor

After you have checked the appropriate boxes above, move to the next section, entitled Your Own. Check any of the boxes below for which your reaction is influenced by a factor listed above. For example, does grooming matter because of your own *comfort level* with someone who is not hygienic? If so, check it. Does promptness, or the lack of it, influence you because of a *negative past experience* of being kept waiting yourself? If so, check it.

Your Own

☐ Comfort level	☐ Own life situations
☐ "Gut" feeling	☐ Negative past experience
☐ Patience/Impatience	☐ Pessimistic future prediction
☐ Personal feelings about the group (e.g., immigrants)	☐ Other _____

Directions for Using Comments and Behaviors That May Indicate Stereotypes and Prejudice

Objectives

- To gain awareness about how behaviors and comments are seen or interpreted.

- To audit the climate and dynamics of the workplace.

- To discuss the impact of these behaviors and comments on the culture of the organization.

- To recognize that the assumptions we make and the ways we behave and talk have consequences on the climate of the workplace.

Intended Audience

- All employees at any level of the organization.

- An intact work group desiring to improve its climate and dynamics.

- Trainers, OD consultants, and HR professionals who are working with or teaching other people in the organization.

Time

- 45 minutes.

Materials

- Copies of Comments and Behaviors That May Indicate Stereotypes and Prejudice worksheet for all participants.

- Pens or pencils.

- Easel, newsprint pad, and felt-tipped markers.

- A copy of the worksheet on a newsprint sheet.

Suggested Procedures

- Introduce the activity by explaining that stereotypes operate much like second-hand smoke, influencing us even if we don't subscribe to them. This activity will help bring to light some of the comments and behaviors that contribute to the "second-hand smoke effect" in the workplace.

- Distribute the worksheet to all participants and have everyone fill it out.

- Explain the directions for scoring and ask people to score their own worksheets.

- Ask participants to form small groups of five to seven members to share responses and discuss what they've seen and heard at the hospital or medical center.

- Take a group profile and record all the "frequently," "occasionally," and "rarely" responses for each item on the newsprint sheet.

- End with a total group discussion that focuses on ways to minimize stereotypes in the organization.

Discussion Questions

- Which comments or behaviors were checked most often?

- How often do these comments or behaviors occur? How widespread are they at your hospital or medical center?

- Which groups seem to be the target of most of the stereotyping?

- What is the effect of these comments and behaviors on patient service? On employee interactions? On perpetuating stereotypes? On condoning ridicule?

- How do you respond when you hear these comments or see these behaviors? What is the result?

- What is the most difficult part of responding when you hear or see these comments or behaviors?

- What can you do to deal with these stereotypical attitudes and prejudicial behaviors when directed at other staff members? What can you do when the subject of comments or behavior is a patient?

- What are the consequences of doing nothing? What can you personally do to ensure that something is done to improve the situation?

Caveats, Considerations, and Adaptations

- Divide the group into five small groups and give each group one item for discussion from "comments" and one from "behaviors."

- Break groups up for discussion based on what the data show and how many people are in the session.

- Tallying and posting participant responses can be omitted to save time.

- Participants may find it difficult to see how these behaviors hinder service to diverse customers, so it is important to spend time discussing the effect of stereotyping on their interactions and the impact on patients and families in very concrete ways. Resistance may signal a need for continued work.

💾 COMMENTS AND BEHAVIORS THAT MAY INDICATE STEREOTYPES AND PREJUDICE

Directions: Read the Comments Heard and Behaviors Seen on the sheet below. Place a ✓ in the appropriate column indicating the degree these are heard or seen in your organization.

Comments Heard	Frequently	Occasionally	Rarely
1. This is America. Why don't they learn to speak English?			
2. They are so cliquish. They all stick together.			
3. This place has really changed. It lacks the old family feeling it used to have.			
4. Why do they have to bring the whole tribe?			
5. I know we're supposed to respect diversity, but some of their customs are weird.			
Behaviors Seen			
1. A lack of cooperation between various departments and/or professional groups.			
2. Avoidance of working or interacting with people of different ages, races, ethnicity, gender, etc.			
3. A lack of diversity in new hires and promotions.			
4. Complaints of unequal treatment of different groups.			
5. Resistance to learning the norms and language of your expanding immigrant patient base.			

Directions for Scoring

Score your worksheet by giving 1 point to each comment you hear or behavior you see "frequently," 2 points to each that you hear or see "occasionally," and 3 points to each that you have "rarely" heard or seen. Place the numbers in the boxes above and then add the points for Comments Heard and Behaviors Seen.

Subtotal Heard:	Subtotal Seen:	Total Points:

The closer your total is to 30 points, the fewer indicators of stereotypes and prejudice exist in your organization. Use the sheet as a way to focus your discussion on opportunities for improvement.

Directions for Using From a Different Perspective

Objectives

- To develop awareness and understanding about those who belong to a different group.

- To gain an understanding about different realities that people experience.

- To broaden views about the multiple factors that shape us all and realize how entrenched misperceptions can become.

Intended Audience

- Staff who work with diverse patients.

- Physicians serving diverse patients.

- Managers of patient service departments.

Time

- 30 to 45 minutes.

Materials

- Copies of the From a Different Perspective worksheet for all participants.

- Pens or pencils.

- Easel, newsprint pad, and felt-tipped markers (optional).

Suggested Procedures

- Distribute the worksheet to each participant and go over the directions.

- Have each individual fill out a worksheet, then pair up and discuss it with another participant.

- Lead a whole group discussion that focuses on what individuals learned and what difference any of these insights might make when dealing with patients in the future.

Discussion Questions

- What identity did you choose? Why?

- What kind of assumptions did you need to make in order to even check the boxes?

- If you were at all uncomfortable during any part of the activity, when did you feel uncomfortable and why?

- What misperceptions did you make about others?

- Where are you subject to misperceptions by others?

- What was your biggest gain from going through this exercise?

- How might your new awareness impact your behavior on the job?

Caveats, Considerations, and Adaptations

- This activity can be done by a work group by first identifying certain populations dealt with at a hospital or medical center. For example, an entire team might do the exercise as though it were part of a Gypsy tribe. The variety of perceptions about how one's life would be the same or different would lead to a good group discussion.

- Identities that reflect the whole variety of your patient population can be assigned to small groups so that each significant population is represented. A spokesperson for each group can then tell that group's perceptions about what would be the same and what would be different. The whole group can respond to each subgroup's perceptions.

- Cards with identities (for example: "You are a 30-year-old woman, a recent immigrant from El Salvador, who is a single parent with three children") can be prepared in advance. Participants can choose cards and respond from the perspective of the person described on the card.

💾 FROM A DIFFERENT PERSPECTIVE

Directions: Imagine that you wake up tomorrow as a patient who is of another gender and group (e.g., ethnic, religious, social, etc.) in your community. What attitudes, values, and beliefs might be the same? What would be different?

	Same	Different
1. Comfort with high-technology tools.		
2. Partnership/relationship with physicians.		
3. Attitudes about having a female physician.		
4. Specific dietary requirements due to religious beliefs.		
5. Views about life and death.		
6. Decision making regarding your treatment.		
7. Preferred health care provider.		
8. Where you would receive your health care.		
9. What would matter to you in terms of patient care.		
10. Accommodations you would expect for family.		
11. The role of the mystical or supernatural in your healing.		
12. Desire to bring home remedies and alternate food choices to the hospital.		

Directions for Using Systemic Points of Contact: Where Stereotypes Can Have an Impact

Objectives

- To raise awareness about and compare employee perceptions of systemic road blocks influenced by stereotypes.

- To use data as a catalyst for system changes.

- To gather data and input that can be distributed throughout the organization.

Intended Audience

- Executives and managers who can make changes to the system.

- Staff at all levels of the organization who can give input.

- Any OD personnel, HR professional, or trainer trying to help an organization accomplish change from within.

- External trainers and consultants trying to help clients open systems.

Time

- 2 hours.

Materials

- Copies of the Systemic Points of Contact: Where Stereotypes Can Have an Impact worksheet for all participants.

- Pens or pencils.

- Easel, newsprint pad, felt-tipped markers, and masking tape for each subgroup.

Suggested Procedures

- Distribute the worksheet and have each person do his or her own analysis of each area, including a description of the situation, the assumptions he or she makes, and a suggestion for improvement. Give people 15 to 20 minutes.

- Put participants in small groups, preferably with five to seven people, to share their perceptions and suggestions for improvement.

- After a few minutes of sharing, ask groups to compare their answers and to come up with their top three suggestions for improvement. Give them about 40 minutes.

- At the end of the 40 minutes, ask a spokesperson for each group to give a short 2-minute overview of the situation as they saw it, then state their three specific suggestions. Limit each small group presentation to 5 minutes.

- List all the suggestions on newsprint for the group.

- Lead a group discussion of the data and help the group decide on next steps to take.

Discussion Questions

- What do you see in the system that gets in the way of full commitment and productivity?

- What did you see or hear from others that surprised you?

- What needs to be changed, and what are the consequences if no changes are made?

- How can you ensure that necessary changes will be made?

Caveats, Considerations, and Adaptations

- This can be an invaluable needs assessment tool for executives who want to know how the organization is seen and experienced by employees.

- This is a good executive retreat activity. Executives can compare their own perceptions of reality, but the biggest gain will come from hearing employees' perceptions and suggestions.

🖫 SYSTEMIC POINTS OF CONTACT: WHERE STEREOTYPES CAN HAVE AN IMPACT

Directions: Consider your organization as you analyze the systems listed below. Examples are given for the hiring and promotion systems, but those are only two of many. You can add to or modify those and fill in others as well.

System	Situation What do I see?	Assumption What do I assume?	Suggestion What do we need to do about it?
Hiring	1) Pursuing an affirmative action style quota system. 2) Reaching out to nontraditional sources for excellent candidates.	1) Diverse hires are less qualified and cannot achieve without help. 2) Breadth of background and experience opens people's eyes and minds.	1) Clarify difference between affirmative action and valuing diversity; help people understand assumptions and biases. 2) Identify good places—traditional and nontraditional—to recruit.
Promotion	Administrative staff is entirely white and male.	If you're not white and male, you don't have a chance. Managers promote clones.	Groom people of many backgrounds, talents, experiences. Develop a coaching and mentoring system that focuses on polishing internal talent.
Hiring			
Promotion			

	Situation	Assumption	Suggestion
System	**What do I see?**	**What do I assume?**	**What do we need to do about it?**
Retention			
Career Planning			
Mentoring			
Succession Planning			
Flexible Benefits			
Other			

Directions for Using You As the Object of Stereotypes

Objectives

- To gain a sense of how others might perceive you, based on various dimensions of diversity.

- To develop empathy for others who are stereotyped by gaining a sense of how it feels to be labeled.

- To explore how the perceptions of others can limit people.

Intended Audience

- All employees in a hospital, clinic, or medical center.

- Members of any team or work group who may inadvertently be limiting one another.

- Managers trying to develop a high-performance team.

Time

- 40 minutes.

Materials

- Copies of the You As the Object of Stereotypes worksheet for all participants.

- Pens or pencils.

- Paper for participants.

- Easel and newsprint sheets.

- Felt-tipped markers.

Suggested Procedures

- Begin by giving a lecturette on stereotypes and perceptions based on material in Chapter 6 of *Managing Diversity in Health Care*. Pay particular attention to the perceptions of others and how limiting they might be.

- Introduce the You As the Object of Stereotypes worksheet. Explain the directions using the sample sheet as an illustration.

- Have each individual fill out his or her own worksheet, listing as many factors as they would like, up to eight.

- After participants have filled out their worksheets, have them pair up and discuss what they wrote.

Discussion Questions

- How easy or difficult was it to identify areas in which you might be stereotyped? (If participants are stuck, have them refer to the Four Layers of Diversity in Chapter 2 of *Managing Diversity in Health Care.)*

- What was your reaction to seeing how others might label or limit you?

- Where do you feel misjudged? Can you do anything about it? If so, what?

- When have you made the same types of misjudgments about other people?

- How can you, as an individual, and how can the organization collectively create an environment in which people can reach their full potential, rather than be limited by the views of others?

Caveats, Considerations, and Adaptations

- Any time you deal with stereotypes and perceptions, you are dealing with potentially painful and volatile subject matter. Set the exercise up by helping participants realize that all people are misjudged and labeled and all misjudge and label others. Being conscious about how that happens can minimize the negative effects.

YOU AS THE OBJECT OF STEREOTYPES (SAMPLE)

Note: This example is for trainer use on either overhead transparency or easel and chart pad. It is not for distribution to participants.

Directions: In each of the spaces below, identify factors around which others may stereotype you. The areas for stereotyping are vast and can range from field of work or level within the organization to skin color, gender, age, marital status, or geographic region. Then jot down the stereotypical assumptions that might be held about you because of that factor. The point of this exercise is to see where you might be limited by the perception others have about you.

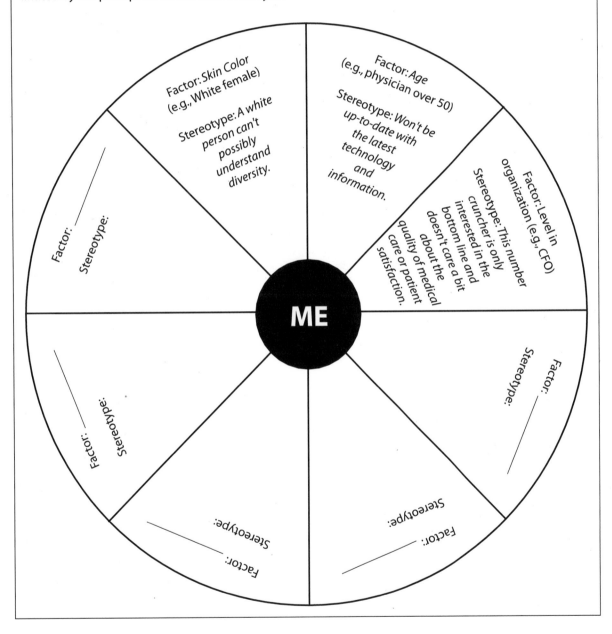

YOU AS THE OBJECT OF STEREOTYPES

Directions: In each of the spaces below, identify factors around which others may stereotype you. The areas for stereotyping are vast and can range from field of work or level within the organization to skin color, gender, age, marital status, or geographic region. Then jot down the stereotypical assumptions that might be held about you because of that factor. The point of this exercise is to see where you might be limited by the perception others have about you.

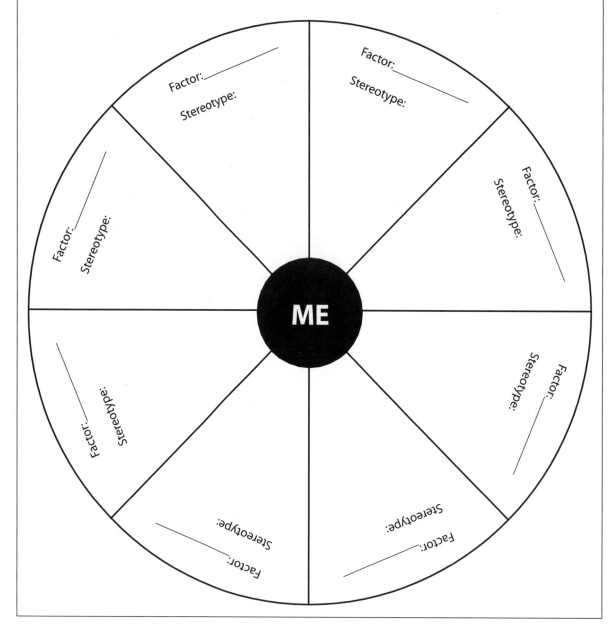

Chapter 10

The Diversity Leadership Challenge

ACCOMPLISHING LONG-TERM CULTURE CHANGE in any organization is at best difficult. To do so in health care organizations, which are in a very fluid industry, ups the ante and often makes accomplishing positive changes more difficult.

One thing is certain. For successful change to happen, effective leadership is essential. So is a clear understanding of the organization's current reality and where it wants to go. This chapter provides a number of assessment tools for leadership characteristics and the culture or climate of an organization. More can be learned about this topic by reading Chapter 7 in *Managing Diversity in Health Care*.

Directions for Using the Diversity Accountability Questionnaire

Objectives

- To assess the practices and responsiveness to diversity throughout an organization.

- To identify tangible signs of a diversity-friendly organization.

- To suggest areas for improvement.

Intended Audience

- Employees at all levels of an organization.

- Managers trying to sensitize a team to diversity-related issues.

- Patient service representatives.

- A CEO or executives leading a discussion of the status of diversity in the organization.

- Any trainer or consultant needing a warm-up or quick needs assessment to start a dialogue.

Time
- 30 to 45 minutes.

Materials
- Copies of the Diversity Accountability Questionnaire for all participants.
- Pens or pencils.
- Easel, newsprint pad, and felt-tipped markers.

Suggested Procedures
- Have each person fill out a copy of the questionnaire and score it.
- Explain that the closer to 40 points an organization is perceived to be, the more accountable it is to a pluralistic employee and patient population. It is helpful for an organization to obtain a wide array of perspectives and to assess the range of perceptions about how most employees experience life in the organization. When used as an assessment tool, the Diversity Accountability Questionnaire can be a catalyst to begin the change process.
- Ask participants to form small groups and discuss each of the items and what the data suggests about the organization's responsiveness.
- Have everyone share perceptions in a whole group discussion.

Discussion Questions
- Which questions need clarification?
- On which ones would you like to make a comment?
- Which were difficult to answer?
- Are there any that "pushed your buttons" or any to which you had very strong responses?
- What do these data suggest about your organization's openness, responsiveness, and flexibility regarding diversity?
- What will it cost if the organization is not more flexible?
- What suggestions came up for what we need to do?
- What is one step you personally can take to create a more diversity friendly culture?

Caveats, Considerations, and Adaptations
- Items can be changed or adapted to suit your organization.
- Although this can be a meaningful centerpiece for any meeting, it can also be a warm-up activity at an all-day session on diversity. It will give you entree to raise issues.

💾 DIVERSITY ACCOUNTABILITY QUESTIONNAIRE

Directions: Focus on your organization as you read the following ten questions. Then place a check mark in the appropriate column.

Questions	Almost Always	Often	Sometimes	Almost Never
1. Bicultural/bilingual staff is hired to reflect the population served.				
2. Patient materials match the languages of the patient base.				
3. Products and services are designed with help from community liaisons.				
4. Resources are utilized to educate employees about cross-cultural norms of the communities served.				
5. Employees from all backgrounds eat, joke, and talk together.				
6. All signs are English only, despite a multilingual population.				
7. Managers are held accountable for building cohesive diverse teams.				
8. The board is selected without paying attention to having community population represented.				
9. Employees are open to learning about and caring for ethnic populations different from their own.				
10. There is a genuine curiosity about and an appreciation for ethnic and religious differences.				

Directions for Scoring

Score numbers 1 through 5, 7, 9, and 10 in the following way:

Almost Always = 4   Often = 3   Sometimes = 2   Almost Never = 1

Score numbers 6 and 8 in the following way:

Almost Always = 1   Often = 2   Sometimes = 3   Almost Never = 4

1. ___   2. ___   3. ___   4. ___   5. ___   6. ___   7. ___   8. ___   9. ___   10. ___   Total: ___

The closer the score is to a 40-point total, the more an organization is perceived to be accountable for maintaining a pluralistic employee and patient population.

Directions for Using Creating a Climate That Results in Top Performance and High Morale

Objectives

- To identify indications of high or low morale throughout the organization.

- To gather needs assessment data indicating where organizational climate needs to be strengthened.

Intended Audience

- A top-management group that wants to stimulate discussion about perceptions of morale and how to strengthen it.

- Managers of diverse work groups who want to improve staff morale.

- Trainers who teach managers elements of a high morale climate.

- Staff at all levels.

Time

- 45 to 60 minutes.

Materials

- Copies of the Creating a Climate That Results in Top Performance and High Morale worksheet for all participants.

- Pens or pencils.

- Easel, newsprint pad, and felt-tipped markers.

Suggested Procedures

- Begin by asking what factors or behaviors are essential for a high morale climate. Have the group brainstorm these while you chart the responses.

- Introduce the questionnaire by stating its purpose and giving directions.

- When they are finished, go over the directions for scoring, asking people to count the "almost always" checks and explaining that the more of these they see, the better the climate.

- Put people in small groups and ask them to discuss the items they think most violate a high morale climate.

- Bring everyone back for a whole group discussion.

Discussion Questions

- Which "almost always" answers did there seem to be most agreement on?

- Which "sometimes" or "almost never" answers seem to take the biggest toll on morale?

- What can you do to improve climate one-on-one or in a team if you have limited authority? If nothing changes, then what?

- Where do the biggest differences in perception occur? How do you account for the differences?

- What is the impact on your own morale from some of the low scoring items?

- What one thing will you do differently as a result of this discussion?

Caveats, Considerations, and Adaptations

- Do not use this activity unless there is a commitment at top levels to respond to the information that comes out.

- Acknowledge that morale factors are most often influenced by people at the top. Limits on change are real. Nevertheless, individuals do matter, and they can shape their own reality. What each person does matters.

- Remind people that organizations did not become unresponsive overnight and they won't be fixed that soon either.

🖫 CREATING A CLIMATE THAT RESULTS IN TOP PERFORMANCE AND HIGH MORALE

Directions: Focus on your organization as you read questions 1 through 15. Then place a ✓ in the appropriate column.

	Almost Always	Sometimes	Almost Never
1. Administrators are visible and approachable.			
2. Top level administrators know peoples' names throughout the organization.			
3. Management finds opportunities to acknowledge the unique contributions of all employees in ways that are appropriate for each employee.			
4. Leaders role model an appreciation of different points of view.			
5. Warm, collegial relationships exist between people of diverse backgrounds and levels in the organization.			
6. Employees feel comfortable discussing issues of race, gender, ethnicity, and sexual orientation.			
7. At least several different points of view are considered before important decisions are made.			
8. Leadership and managerial positions reflect diversity.			
9. Employees who want to grow and be promoted can find coaches, advocates, and informal mentors.			
10. People are held accountable for effectively managing differences at their level.			

Source: Adapted with permission from *The Diversity Tool Kit.* © Lee Gardenswartz and Anita Rowe. Burr Ridge, IL: Irwin Professional, 1994.

	Almost Always	Sometimes	Almost Never
11. There is an absence of racial, ethnic, and sexual slurs, jokes, and tension.			
12. All employees are welcome and accepted regardless of lifestyle variations.			
13. Employees have the opportunity to honor and observe their own ethnic or religious customs and holidays.			
14. Diversity is seen as a business issue that can be a competitive advantage.			
15. Benefits have been customized to suit the multiple needs and lifestyle preferences of employees.			

Directions for Scoring

Directions: Score items, then tally the number of responses in each category and record them in the boxes below.

Almost Always	Sometimes	Almost Never

The more "almost always" responses you have, the better the chance that your group's or organization's performance and morale are high. Analyze your "almost never" responses. If there are none, refer to your "sometimes" responses. Determine where your group or organization is vulnerable and think about possible actions that it could take to turn some of those situations around.

Directions for Using the Climate Survey

Objectives

- To gather needs assessment information for feedback.

- To obtain a sense of the organization's climate and feelings about the group.

- To identify strengths and areas for improvement regarding group or organizational climate.

Intended Audience

- Members of ongoing teams and task forces.

- Managers of diverse teams who want to learn about and improve elements of an effective climate.

- Top management groups wanting data about organizational climate. (Data can be collected throughout all or various parts of the organization and shown to top management.)

- Trainers, facilitators, or HR personnel conducting audits or gathering data in an informal way.

Time

- 45 minutes.

Materials

- Copies of the Climate Survey for all participants.

- Pens or pencils.

- Easel, newsprint pad, and felt-tipped markers (optional).

Suggested Procedures

- Begin by having the group brainstorm characteristics of the best organizational climates they have ever been in.

- Distribute the survey and read the directions so that participants take and score their own surveys. Explain that the more "almost always" responses, in general, the healthier the organizational climate.

- Tell participants that the data will be tabulated and shared anonymously with top management.

- Have participants form small groups or pairs to compare and discuss their responses.

- Lead a discussion of issues and insights with the whole group.

Discussion Questions

- What do your responses say about the climate in your work group?

- How do your responses and perceptions compare with those of your co-workers?

- How do any of these factors change in an environment of intense change?

- Do you remember experiencing times of relative stability and, if so, what behaviors characterized that climate?

- Based on your observations, what words of wisdom would you offer leaders at any level trying to maintain a motivating team climate in a time of high anxiety and rapid change?

Caveats, Considerations, and Adaptations

- You can substitute items and add those that seem more relevant to your organization.

- You can break up the list of items and use two or three at a time as warm-ups to meetings about organizational climate.

- You could adapt the scoring to reflect numbers 1, 2, 3, 4, and 5, with five being "high climate and morale."

💾 CLIMATE SURVEY

Directions: Identify the work group with whom you most associate and interact. Then respond to the questions below with the most appropriate answer. Once you have responded, you can see where your group's climate is thriving, where it also might be sagging, and under what conditions.

Questions	Almost Always	Sometimes	Almost Never
1. The environment is easy and comfortable, even when discussing thorny issues.			
2. Enthusiasm and participation around here is high.			
3. New, unconventional ideas are encouraged.			
4. Different points of view on any issue are welcome and applauded.			
5. Many ideas are cultivated; none are ridiculed.			
6. People share their ideas openly.			
7. It is no secret where everyone stands on the issues that come up; people state their positions.			
8. There is respect for principles of others, even in the face of disagreement.			
9. Clarifying, and sometimes challenging, questions are expected and asked in unhostile tones.			
10. Positions change as a result of discussions on the issues.			
11. Feedback is given frequently and constructively.			
12. Relevant and appropriate self-disclosure on any pertinent issue is given.			
13. Group members build on the ideas of others and collaborate willingly.			
14. There is confidence in the group's ability to do the job.			
15. Individual and collective accountability is a high priority.			

Directions for Scoring

Tally the number of "almost always," "sometimes," and "almost never" responses. Record the numbers in the boxes below. Generally, the more "almost always" answers, the more the organization's climate is thriving.

Almost Always	Sometimes	Almost Never

After assessing your responses, find the top two items that could sabotage your group's climate. Write these two items and one thing you can personally do about each on the back of this sheet.

Directions for Using the Leadership Characteristics Questionnaire

Objectives

- To assess one's competencies and effectiveness as a leader.

- To identify areas for growth and improvement.

- To generate discussion among staff about what constitutes excellent leadership.

Intended Audience

- Executive or managerial staff evaluating individual and collective leadership of staff members.

- Organization development consultants, trainers, and facilitators helping develop leaders.

- Human resource personnel who coach leaders and managers.

Time

- 45 minutes.

Materials

- Copies of the Leadership Characteristics Questionnaire for each participant.

- Pens and pencils.

- Easel, newsprint pad, and felt-tipped markers.

Suggested Procedures

- Distribute questionnaires to participants. Ask them to rate themselves honestly regarding how often they practice each of the leadership factors listed.

- Explain that the more "almost always" responses they have, the more they show these ten leadership characteristics.

- Ask them to form pairs or threesomes to obtain feedback on these same factors from people who know them well.

- Lead a large group discussion of the ten characteristics and ask what else should be added to the list. Chart suggestsions on newsprint in front of the group.

Discussion Questions

- What do the results of the questionnaire and your discussion in small groups say about your leadership strengths?

- Do you think the results accurately reflect your tendencies?

- Where do you need to grow?

- Would you add anything else to the list? If so, what?

- Consider your leadership team. Which of the factors are covered? What does the leadership group need to work on?

- From whom can you obtain feedback to check out your assumptions about yourself?

Caveats, Considerations, and Adaptations

- Although the questionnaire was designed as an individual assessment tool, it can also be a team tool. For example, an executive team can discuss its performance as a group in each of the ten areas, then discuss where they need to adapt or change. Build on that beginning by going around the group to see who has strengths in each area. This is a rich exercise when done in a whole group with colleagues offering one another feedback. Write down the names of those who most reflect each characteristic. Then identify what's missing on the team and discuss how to develop that factor.

- End by giving each person feedback about where he or she most needs to grow and asking everyone to make action plans. This is especially powerful if you chart the names and responses of each person. Making responses public is a way to build support between co-workers and bolster accountability.

🖫 LEADERSHIP CHARACTERISTICS QUESTIONNAIRE

Directions: To assess your own competence and effectiveness as a leader in a health care institution, respond as honestly and accurately as possible to how much the following factors reflect your leadership.

	Almost Always	Sometimes	Almost Never
1. Being meaning driven.			
2. Taking a long view of results.			
3. Demonstrating commitment through investing resources.			
4. Basing decisions on the core values of the organization.			
5. Engaging in creative, open-minded thinking.			
6. Demanding accountability for results, but offering flexibility in accomplishment.			
7. Being willing to change, grow, and adapt.			
8. Creating an environment that questions assumptions, systems, and processes.			
9. Encouraging risks and breaking new ground.			
10. Investing in relationships with people.			

Directions for Using Leadership Characteristics Questionnaire Assessment

Objectives

- To enable each person to explore his or her strengths and weaknesses for leadership.

- To develop action plans to go beyond discussion to the commitment stage.

- To reinforce strengths and add to skill sets.

Intended Audience

- Leaders and managers at any level of the organization.

- Any HR professional, trainer, facilitator, or consultant charged with the responsibility to teach, groom, and grow leaders.

Time

- 30 minutes.

Materials

- Copies of their completed Leadership Characteristics Questionnaires and copies of the Leadership Characteristics Questionnaire Assessment worksheets for all participants.

- Pens or pencils.

Suggested Procedures

- First refresh people's memory about their results from the questionnaire.

- Hand out the assessment sheets.

- Ask participants to work with a boss, coach, mentor, co-worker, or someone whom they trust and ask for feedback from that person on the questionnaire.

- Tell participants to work together in their pairs to decide how they can reinforce their strengths and to come up with a plan for improving their weaknesses.

Discussion Questions

- What do your questionnaire results indicate?

- Based on that data, what is a reasonable action plan for you?

- How will you hold yourself accountable for completing your plan?

- When can we meet again to do follow-up?

Caveats, Considerations, and Adaptations

- This questionnaire can be added to coaching, grooming, or mentoring programs.

- Items can be changed, added, or deleted.

💾 LEADERSHIP CHARACTERISTICS QUESTIONNAIRE ASSESSMENT

Directions: After assessing your leadership strengths, explore these ten items in more detail. Focus particularly on your "almost always" and "almost never" categories.

Characteristics	What I Can Do to Reinforce My Strengths	What I Can Do to Improve My Weaknesses
• Being meaning driven.		
• Taking a long view of results.		
• Demonstrating commitment through investing resources.		
• Basing decisions on the core values of the organization.		
• Engaging in creative, open-minded thinking.		
• Demanding accountability for results, but offering flexibility in accomplishment.		
• Being willing to change, grow, and adapt.		
• Creating an environment that questions assumptions, systems, and processes.		
• Encouraging risks and breaking new ground.		
• Investing in relationships with people.		

Source: Used with permission from *Lending and Diversity Handbook.* © Lee Gardenswartz and Anita Rowe. Burr Ridge, IL: Irwin Professional, 1997.

Directions for Using Diversity: Staff Expectation Survey

Objectives

- To assess employee perceptions, expectations, and readiness regarding diversity.

- To gather data to utilize in designing a diversity initiative.

Intended Audience

- All employees or a random selection of employees who reflect horizontal, diagonal, and vertical slices of the organization.

- Teams, task forces, or work groups.

- Managers who want data about their teams.

- Trainers, facilitators, or consultants who want to show managers how to conduct a needs assessment.

Time

- 45 minutes.

Materials

- Copies of the Diversity: Staff Expectation Survey for all participants.

- Pens or pencils.

- Easel, newsprint pad, and felt-tipped markers.

Suggested Procedures

- Introduce the questionnaire by stating the rationale for administering it, what will happen to the data, by when, and for whom. Be sure to guarantee anonymity if you want them returned.

- Collect data, tally up the scores, and average them.

- If administered in a group, list each item with the average score and the range on a newsprint sheet; then lead a discussion about the results.

Discussion Questions

- What do the results indicate about the organization's (or team's) readiness, perceptions, and expectations regarding diversity?

- If employees, patients, and families are truly to feel welcome, what needs to change here?

- What surprises you in the data you see?

- How do you account for the wide range of responses?

- Where do we go from here?

Caveats, Considerations, and Adaptations

- Change any items to more clearly reflect the reality of your facility.

- It takes time to tally the scores and make the chart. If the survey is used during a training session, collect the data and move the group into the next learning activity. While they work on the learning activity, you or a co-trainer can score the survey and compute averages. You can also send the survey out ahead of time and compute the data prior to the session.

- Make sure the group is large enough (at least seven or eight people) so that anonymity is guaranteed.

💾 **DIVERSITY: STAFF EXPECTATION SURVEY**

Directions: Respond to items 1 through 12 by circling the appropriate number. There is no right answer, only your answer, honestly given, based on your perception. Data will be reported collectively so the anonymity of each person is assured.

---

1. The staff is clear about our organization's goals and priorities regarding diversity.

1	2	3	4	5
Rarely		Sometimes		Almost always

---

2. Employees feel that they have influence in setting priorities and making decisions, particularly those that affect them.

1	2	3	4	5
Rarely		Sometimes		Almost always

---

3. Employees understand the need for and buy into diversity education as a tool for learning how to treat patients and one another better.

1	2	3	4	5
Rarely		Sometimes		Almost always

---

4. We have a climate in which it is safe to express values and ideas, no matter how they differ.

1	2	3	4	5
Rarely		Sometimes		Almost always

---

5. Employees are clear about their roles and responsibilities, internally and externally.

1	2	3	4	5
Rarely		Sometimes		Almost always

---

6. There is an environment of openness and inclusion, suggesting that any patient would feel welcome here.

1	2	3	4	5
Rarely		Sometimes		Almost always

---

7. We not only tolerate but value the differences people bring to the workplace.

1	2	3	4	5
Rarely		Sometimes		Almost always

---

8. Expectations for employees regarding ways to serve a complex patient base effectively are clear.

1	2	3	4	5
Rarely		Sometimes		Almost always

---

9. Employees are rewarded for taking risks and showing initiative.

1	2	3	4	5
Rarely		Sometimes		Almost always

---

10. People at all levels of the organization can be trusted to come through on their jobs.

1	2	3	4	5
Rarely		Sometimes		Almost always

---

11. Our organization has a meaningful role in the life of our community.

1	2	3	4	5
Rarely		Sometimes		Almost always

---

12. At work I can show who I really am and still succeed.

1	2	3	4	5
Rarely		Sometimes		Almost always

Chapter 11

Overcoming Barriers to Change

CHANGE, EVEN WHEN IT IS DESIRED, IS CHALLENGING. The process of helping people leave the familiar for the unknown is difficult because it goes against the basic desire that humans have for predictability and security. This chapter provides tools that enable the trainer to identify and understand resistance to change at a conceptual and practical level, while simultaneously helping participants understand the need for it and create vehicles to make change happen. For more understanding about creating change and overcoming barriers to it, see Chapter 8 in *Managing Diversity in Health Care.*

Directions for Using Testing Commitment from the Top

Objectives

- To assess the strength of the CEO and his or her top executive staff's commitment to diversity.

- To generate discussion about how commitment from them would be demonstrated.

- To help staff charged with responsibility for diversity know what to ask leaders for, such as time, visibility on the issue, and resources.

- To identify concrete behaviors that indicate support.

- To gather data about staff perceptions of conditions and commitment to diversity.

Intended Audience

- Executives and leaders of diverse organizations.
- Diversity task forces charged with implementing diversity.
- Human resource personnel, external consultants, or those in charge of diversity efforts.

Time

- 40 minutes.

Materials

- Copies of Testing Commitment from the Top for all participants.
- Pens or pencils.

Suggested Procedures

- Distribute the worksheets and ask participants to fill them out.
- Discuss the results, first looking at "I can count on it" answers.
- Then lead a discussion of "not sure" and "not yet" responses.
- Finally, lead a discussion around needed changes and how progress can be made.

Discussion Questions

- What about this data makes you feel hopeful?
- Is there anything alarming or disappointing in the results?
- If so, what can you do to influence commitment for change?
- Is there anything that surprised you about the results?
- Are there any other indicators of commitment that you would like to add?

Caveats, Considerations, and Adaptations

- Data about perceptions of commitment can be collected and fed upward to executives.
- You can either compare executives' collective perceptions with those of the rest of the organization or just feed up the data you have. The first idea is more interesting and engaging. It serves as a reality check and a prescription for what it means to give and actually demonstrate support.
- Obstacles identified can be the focus of problem solving and action planning.

💾 TESTING COMMITMENT FROM THE TOP

Directions: Read the items below and put a ✓ in the appropriate columns.

Item	I Can Count on It	Not Sure	Not Yet
1. Our CEO and other executives talk frequently about diversity's strategic importance.			
2. Our top leadership team models appreciation of diversity in its membership.			
3. Visible top leader support is shown in speeches, newsletters, and other communication vehicles.			
4. Time is made to talk to employees at all levels to help them understand diversity issues in our organization.			
5. Sensitivity to needs is demonstrated through flextime policies.			
6. Holidays, symbols, celebrations, and rituals of many groups are honored and respected here.			
7. There are many ways to do things here, not just one. Flexibility is highly prized.			
8. The performance review of all employees has diversity-related measures.			
9. Top leadership demonstrates a knowledge of different cultural norms in its behavior.			
10. Executive members serve on task force teams and/or attend training to demonstrate commitment.			

Directions for Using Serving Diverse Patients and Families: An Assessment Questionnaire

Objectives

- To assess the diversity friendliness of your facility in serving a wide array of patients.

- To use the data as leverage to improve and legitimize a diversity initiative.

- To raise awareness about needed areas of improvement.

Intended Audience

- Employees at all levels of the organization.

- Managers of staff serving diverse patients.

- Consultants, trainers, and HR personnel leading customer service, long-term change, or diversity initiatives.

Time

- 60 minutes.

Materials

- Copies of Serving Diverse Patients and Families: An Assessment Questionnaire for all participants.

- Pens or pencils.

- Easel, newsprint pad, and felt-tipped markers.

Suggested Procedures

- Distribute the questionnaire and ask each person to answer honestly based on the part of the organization they see.

- Have participants score their questionnaires and then explain the three concepts the questionnaire is evaluating: (1) services, (2) systems, and (3) relationships.

- Tell participants to form small groups and discuss questions that you list on the easel in front of the room.

- Lead a wrap-up discussion with the entire group and conclude with a commitment to next steps.

Discussion Questions

- In which of the three areas (services, systems, or relationships) do you see your greatest strength?

- Where does your competition do better than you? How do you know?

- What do you have to do better? Differently?

- How will you make the needed changes happen?

Caveats, Considerations, and Adaptations

- Change items and tailor them for your audience, but make certain they fit into the three concepts. For example, substitute one question that measures service for another question that measures service.

💾 SERVING DIVERSE PATIENTS AND FAMILIES: AN ASSESSMENT QUESTIONNAIRE

Directions: Rate your hospital by placing a check in the appropriate column.

		Very True	Sometimes True	Not True
1.	We learn about the customs of others to meet the needs of our patients.	☐	☐	☐
2.	We have alternate methods of communicating with and helping our patients.	☐	☐	☐
3.	Resources are spent to educate employees about cross-cultural norms of our community population.	☐	☐	☐
4.	We solicit and receive feedback from patients about their treatment and care.	☐	☐	☐
5.	Employees are rewarded for specific behaviors that make people feel welcome.	☐	☐	☐
6.	Patients are treated with dignity and respect.	☐	☐	☐
7.	We are aware of genetic predispositions of the populations we serve.	☐	☐	☐
8.	Employees are encouraged to find ways to respect the traditions and beliefs of all the patients.	☐	☐	☐
9.	Employees have good interpersonal communication skills.	☐	☐	☐
10.	We know enough about the needs and preferences of community members to offer patient care in an appropriate fashion.	☐	☐	☐
11.	We have people to consult as resources when we need to learn more about different groups in our community.	☐	☐	☐
12.	Hospital administrators participate in community organizations and functions.	☐	☐	☐

		Very True	Sometimes True	Not True
13.	Management spends time learning new skills to manage a wider array of people.	☐	☐	☐
14.	We have alternate ways to help people in crisis.	☐	☐	☐
15.	Employees have been trained in customer service and communication skills.	☐	☐	☐
16.	We can effectively accommodate non-English speakers.	☐	☐	☐
17.	Management has made it clear that diversity is a top priority.	☐	☐	☐
18.	Employees are open to serving ethnic populations different from their own.	☐	☐	☐

Directions for Scoring

Use the following scoring key for all items and place the total score in categories, as shown below:

Very True = 2   Sometimes True = 1   Not True = 0

Items 1, 4, 7, 10, 13, 16	Services	Points _____
Items 2, 5, 8, 11, 14, 17	Systems	Points _____
Items 3, 6, 9, 12, 15, 18	Relationships	Points _____

Interpretation of Scores

The questionnaire evaluates customer service in three areas: (1) services available to accommodate a pluralistic population; (2) systems in place to encourage excellent service for a wide array of patients; and (3) relationships developed across all parts of the community.

The higher the score, the better an organization serves its broad patient base. Items with low scores offer important feedback and provide starting points for meaningful change. Use the results to determine action plans for improvement.

Directions for Using Managing Diversity Questionnaire

Objectives

- To assess three levels of an organization's effectiveness in managing a diverse workforce: individual attitudes, organizational values, and management practices.

- To increase awareness and knowledge about aspects of managing diversity.

- To target areas of needed development.

Intended Audience

- Staff at all levels in an organization.

- Executives, middle management, and/or diversity councils involved in planning diversity development strategies.

- Executive staff members charged with organizational strategy regarding diversity.

- Trainees in a managing diversity seminar.

Time

- 45 minutes.

Materials

- Copies of the Managing Diversity Questionnaire for all participants.

- Pens or pencils.

Suggested Procedures

- Give all participants copies of the questionnaire and ask them to fill them out based on their perceptions of the organization and how it functions.

- Emphasize that responses are anonymous and ask them to be candid; explain how the results will be used, who will see them, and what will be done with them.

- Ask participants to score their own questionnaires and then collect them.

- Compile and analyze the results by item, by the three levels of functioning, and by demographic groupings of staff.

- Report the data to appropriate executive and or management staff.

- Communicate a summary of findings to all participants, along with an indication of next steps.

- Lead the participants themselves or those who receive the data in a discussion of results and next steps based on their answers to the discussion questions.

Discussion Questions

- What are our organization's strengths and weaknesses?

- How similar or disparate are perceptions of different groups, divisions, or levels within the organization?

- What issues need further investigation or clarification?

- What issues need attention?

- Who or what (positions, levels) needs to be involved in dealing with the issues that surfaced?

Caveats, Considerations, and Adaptations

- Do not embark on a process of this type until you have a clear plan about how the data will be used and a commitment from upper management to use the data in planning.

- This questionnaire can be used as an awareness builder for managers who want to increase their own effectiveness in managing diversity and/or for those involved in leading a diversity change process. It can also be used as a jumping-off point for discussions about managing diversity in executive and/or management staff meetings.

- Questionnaires can be coded by level, department, length of time with the company, type of work, and so on to give more specific categories for analysis.

💾 MANAGING DIVERSITY QUESTIONNAIRE

	Very True	Somewhat True	Not True
In this organization:			
1. I am at ease with people of diverse backgrounds.	☐	☐	☐
2. Diverse staff exists at all levels.			
3. Managers have a track record of hiring and promoting diverse employees.	☐	☐	☐
4. In general, I find change stimulating, exciting, and challenging.	☐	☐	☐
5. Racial, ethnic, and gender jokes are tolerated in the informal environment.	☐	☐	☐
6. Managers hold all people equally accountable.	☐	☐	☐
7. I know about the cultural norms of different groups.	☐	☐	☐
8. The formation of ethnic and gender support groups is encouraged.	☐	☐	☐
9. Managers are flexible, structuring benefits and rules that work for everyone.	☐	☐	☐
10. I am afraid to disagree with members of other groups for fear of being called prejudiced.	☐	☐	☐
11. There is a mentoring program that identifies and prepares qualified men and women of all backgrounds for promotion.	☐	☐	☐
12. Appreciation of differences can be seen in the rewards managers give.	☐	☐	☐
13. I feel there is more than one right way to do things.	☐	☐	☐
14. Members of the nondominant group feel they belong.	☐	☐	☐
15. One criterion of a manager's performance review is developing the diversity of his or her staff.	☐	☐	☐
16. I think that diverse viewpoints make for creativity.	☐	☐	☐
17. There is high turnover among women and people of color.	☐	☐	☐

Source: Adapted with permission from *The Managing Diversity Survival Guide.* © Lee Gardenswartz and Anita Rowe. Burr Ridge, IL: Irwin Professional, 1994.

	Very True	Somewhat True	Not True
18. Managers give feedback and evaluate performance so employees do not "lose face."	☐	☐	☐
19. I am aware of my own assumptions and stereotypes.	☐	☐	☐
20. Policies are flexible enough to accommodate everyone.	☐	☐	☐
21. Managers receive active participation from all employees in meetings.	☐	☐	☐
22. I think there is enough common ground to hold staff together.	☐	☐	☐
23. The speaking of other languages is forbidden.	☐	☐	☐
24. Multicultural work teams function harmoniously.	☐	☐	☐
25. Staff members spend their lunch hour and breaks in mixed groups.	☐	☐	☐
26. Money and time are spent on diversity development activities.	☐	☐	☐
27. Managers effectively use problem-solving skills to deal with language differences or other cultural clashes.	☐ ☐	☐ ☐	☐ ☐
28. I feel that working in a diverse staff enriches me.	☐	☐	☐
29. Top management backs up the value it places on diversity with action.	☐	☐	☐
30. Managers have effective strategies to use when one group refuses to work with another.	☐	☐	☐

Directions for Scoring

Items 5, 10, 17, and 23 are scored in the following way:

Very True = 0   Somewhat True = 1   Not True = 2

All other items are scored as follows:

Very True = 2   Somewhat True = 1   Not True = 0

_____ Individual Attitudes and Beliefs (Items 1, 4, 7, 10, 13, 16, 19, 22, 25, 28)

_____ Organizational Values and Norms (Items 2, 5, 8, 11, 14, 17, 20, 24, 26, 29)

_____ Management Practices and Policies (Items 3, 6 9, 12, 15, 18, 21, 24, 27, 30)

_____ Total Score

There are sixty possible points, twenty in each area. The subtotals give an organization an idea of how it is doing in each area. The closer to 20 each score is, the better. Do an item analysis to identify possible areas for improvement.

Directions for Using the Problem-Solving Response Sheet

Objectives

- To gain an awareness about participants' reactions, opinions, strengths, and weaknesses with regard to problem solving.

- To help a problem-solving team or task force learn about one another to solve problems better together.

Intended Audience

- Employees at any level who are working together to solve problems.

- Diversity councils or task forces.

- Trainers or consultants helping groups problem solve.

Time

- 30 minutes.

Materials

- Copies of the Problem-Solving Response Sheet for all participants.

- Pens or pencils.

Suggested Procedures

- Introduce the activity as a way to focus on problem-solving strengths and preferences.

- Hand out copies of the response sheet and pens or pencils.

- Ask participants to pair up and take turns answering the questions following the directions. They do not need to write their answers if they just want to discuss each question orally.

- After 15 minutes, bring participants back to the large group, asking them to share representative answers. Be sure to include question 20.

- Discuss problem solving in general with the group.

Discussion Questions

- Which questions were most interesting? Relevant? Hard to answer?

- What question does this raise or what observations does this help you make regarding yourself as a problem solver?

- What observations can you make about this group? This organization?

- What is your most important insight from your paired discussion? The whole group discussion?

Caveats, Considerations, and Adaptations

- If you are running short of time, be sure that participants discuss question 20.

- Participant can write responses out if they desire. Writing answers may give them more security, but it will also take more time.

- You can substitute items or shorten the list.

- One or two items written on newsprint can be used as a warm-up to a meeting or problem-solving session. Go around the group hearing from everyone on each question that you choose.

💾 PROBLEM-SOLVING RESPONSE SHEET

Directions: The series of open-ended statements is intended to help you discover your reactions to and opinions about problem solving, with particular emphasis on your problem-solving responses and on the way problems are solved in your organization. You will get more out of this exercise if you share it with a partner or share and learn from your whole team.

- Take turns initiating the discussion.
- Complete statements orally.
- Items may be responded to in random order.

1. Problem solving is . . .

2. I am most effective in problem solving when . . .

3. The most difficult diversity-related problems for me to solve are . . .

4. I know I have a good solution when . . .

5. When I'm stumped and need to solve a problem, I . . .

6. The most important consideration in solving a problem is . . .

7. My greatest obstacle in problem solving with people who are different from me is . . .

8. I tend to limit my options by . . .

9. I avoid facing problems when . . .

10. My greatest strength in problem solving is . . .

11. I rush to premature solutions when . . .

12. One thing that inhibits my creative problem solving is . . .

13. In my work group, we solve problems by . . .

14. As a work group, we solve problems by . . .

15. I am most supportive of my boss's solutions when . . .

16. I contribute most in problem solving when . . .

17. I am least likely to implement a solution when . . .

18. Effective problem solving in health care requires . . .

19. In my hospital, the most common method of solving problems is . . .

20. The most difficult problems to solve in this medical center are . . .

Directions for Using Behaviors of an Effective Health Care Employee in a Pluralistic Environment

Objectives

- To stimulate discussion about essential behaviors necessary for employees in a cross-cultural health care environment.

- To define some clear behaviors that managers can teach their staff members.

Intended Audience

- Managers helping coach, groom, or teach employees to be more effective in a cross-cultural environment.

- Trainers, consultants, and HR professionals who work with health care staff.

- High-achieving employees who would like the chance to manage and supervise others.

- Staff who serve diverse patient groups.

Time

- 60 minutes.

Materials

- Copies of Behaviors of an Effective Health Care Employee in a Pluralistic Environment worksheet for all participants.

- Pens or pencils.

- Easel, newsprint pad, and felt-tipped markers.

Suggested Procedures

- Begin by explaining that the health care employee of today who works in a diverse environment needs a refined set of skills different from those of a manager or employee who worked in a homogeneous environment years ago.

- Ask participants to form groups of approximately seven participants each and tell each group where to sit.

- Once groups have formed, hand out the worksheets and explain that each person is to read all ten behaviors that are listed and determine their order of importance from his or her viewpoint, with 1 being most important and 10 being least important.

- After they have had time to think of their rankings, tell people to record their answers in the "Individual Ranking" column.

- Tell groups to discuss their individual rankings with other members of their group, with the goal of reaching consensus on the order. Tell them to record their group answers in the column marked "Group Ranking."

- At this point, you may want to give a few rules for achieving consensus:

  > Consensus is defined as "something we can support for at least some period of time."

  > Each person is responsible for presenting his or her own viewpoint, but not arguing for it.

  > There should be no voting.

  > Keep focusing on common ground and working toward agreement.

- Give the groups approximately 30 minutes to discuss the items and reach consensus.

- Draw a grid on the newsprint pad to record the rankings of all groups and to compare their responses.

- Lead a large group discussion focused on the underlying values of each choice, the range of differences, the strength of people's beliefs, and the ability to be open-minded and able to change.

Discussion Questions

- What was your reaction to participating in this exercise?

- Look at the different responses from each group. What do they mean to you?

- What principles or values guided your choices? Share some of the discussion points that influenced the ranking within your group.

- What health care behaviors might be added to or subtracted from this list if you were in a more homogeneous environment?

- What do these results say to all employees, especially those who would like more knowledge about cultural literacy and its importance for patients and employees?

- What do the results suggest are the "must have" skills for a diverse environment?

- What can you or your team do to develop or enhance your use of these skills?

- Did people change their minds during group discussions? If so, what made that possible? What are the implications of an openness to change on a daily basis?

Caveats, Considerations, and Adaptations

- This is a useful feedback tool for managers who want input from their subordinates or for managers who want to help staff see the importance of cross-cultural knowledge. They can first teach consensus guidelines and then use this tool to gain feedback in an indirect, nonthreatening way while they also develop their subordinates' decision-making skills.

- This can also be used for teaching consensus. The discussion questions, however, would then focus on the group's interaction—how easy or difficult it was to achieve consensus and what behaviors helped or hindered the group in doing so.

- Participants can add behaviors to the list or can brainstorm their own lists before ranking them.

🖫 BEHAVIORS OF AN EFFECTIVE HEALTH CARE EMPLOYEE IN A PLURALISTIC ENVIRONMENT

Directions: Rank order your responses from 1 to 10, 1 being the most important behavior for a health care employee. Then reach consensus as a group on the order of importance from 1 to 10.

Your Ranking		Group Ranking
	Works through religious and various community groups to create ties to the community.	
	Understands the different cultural norms and preferences of patients and co-workers.	
	Takes the initiative to offer information to make patients feel comfortable.	
	Is flexible and creative in finding alternate ways of informing and communicating with patients and families.	
	Cultivates productive relationships with fellow employees.	
	Treats all patients and family members with dignity and respect.	
	Gives necessary information in ways that people of various backgrounds and education levels can understand.	
	Knows how to work within the system to make the process as user friendly as possible.	
	Takes pride in helping patients feel secure.	
	Solicits and uses feedback to improve interactions with patients and families.	

Part Three

Resources

TO INCREASE ONE'S COMPETENCE AS A DIVERSITY TRAINER requires continued acquisition of knowledge and an ongoing exploration of issues. Chapter 12 provides a list of books that trainers can use to grow and learn, answer questions, and stimulate further thinking on the topic of diversity. Included in Chapter 13 are other resources, such as videotapes and games, that can augment the learning activities in this book and add variety and additional approaches to training agendas. These resource listings can also be shared with participants who wish to pursue the topic further.

Chapter 12

Book Resources

THIS CHAPTER PROVIDES AN ANNOTATED LISTING of books on the topic of diversity in the United States today, some specific to the health care setting and others on more general issues, such as gender differences and African Americans, or facilitation and training. The topic areas are sorted alphabetically, beginning with books about African Americans and continuing with those about customer service and marketing, gender, general diversity information, health care, Latinos, other diverse groups, and training and facilitation of diverse groups.

AFRICAN-AMERICAN ISSUES

Chideya, F. (1995). *Don't believe the hype: Fighting cultural misinformation about African-Americans.* New York: Penguin.

This book offers an array of factual information to refute many common misconceptions and stereotypes about African Americans. It is designed to give readers a chance to question the standard depictions of race in today's news media and popular press.

Davis, G., & Watson, G. (1982). *Black life in corporate America.* Garden City, NY: Anchor Press/Doubleday.

This book sheds light on the impact of American organizational culture on black employees.

Fernandez, J. (1981). *Racism and sexism in corporate life.* Lexington, MA: Lexington.

This book discusses the findings of a major study of black and white men and women in the workplace, focusing on how racism and sexism affect their work lives.

Gary, L. (1981). *Black men.* Thousand Oaks, CA: Sage.
This book discusses issues confronting black men in America today.

Grier, W. H., & Cobbs, P. M. (1992). *Black rage.* New York: Basic Books.
This classic in the diversity field offers the views of two black psychiatrists on the inner conflicts and desperation of black life in the United States.

Hacker, A. (1992). *Two nations: Black and white, separate, hostile, unequal.* New York: Scribner's.
A fresh and human analysis of race relations in America is given in this book, which diagnoses the problems, but offers no prescription for solutions.

Rodgers-Rose, L. (1993). *Black women.* Thousand Oaks, CA: Sage.
Issues and conditions confronting black women are discussed in this book.

Taylor, R. J., Jackson, J. S., & Chotters, L. M. (Eds.). (1997). *Family life in black America.* Thousand Oaks, CA: Sage.
This series of articles moves away from a deficit perspective and problem focus and offers information based on empirical data regarding the diversity among today's African-American families.

West, C. (1993). *Race matters.* Boston, MA: Beacon.
In this book the author discusses the dynamics and impact of racism in America.

Williams, G. H. (1995). *Life on the color line.* New York: Dutton.
This true story of a white boy who discovered he was black poignantly illustrates the effects of prejudice and discrimination in American life.

Work, J. W. (1984). *Race, economics and corporate America.* Wilmington, DE: Scholarly Resources.
This book explores the impact of socioeconomic factors and racism on the status of African Americans.

CUSTOMER SERVICE AND MARKETING IN A DIVERSE ENVIRONMENT

Ricks, D. A. (1993). *Blunders in international business.* Cambridge, MA: Blackwell.
This book, based on the premise that mistakes often teach more than successes, focuses on examples of blunders that illustrate the cost of

not understanding cultural differences in business. It is rich with anecdotes and stories that demonstrate the point.

Rossman, M. L. (1994). *Multicultural marketing: Selling to a diverse America.* New York: AMACOM.

In this book the author describes the $500 billion market represented by America's so-called "minorities," the most important consumer growth area in the United States. She then goes on to explain differences among the segments of this market and how to reach them.

Shames, G. W., & Glover, G. W. (1989). *World-class service.* Yarmouth, ME: Intercultural Press.

This book explores the implications of world-class service from four major operational perspectives—business strategy, marketing, human resource development, and customer contact—using specific organizations and cases. It emphasizes cross-cultural management as a key priority in the operational phases of international or domestic cross-cultural business operations.

Thiederman, S. (1991). *Profiting in America's multicultural marketplace: How to do business across cultural lines.* Lexington, MA: Lexington.

In practical, readable terms, the author explains cultural effects on person-to-person behavior and how to communicate effectively with people of different backgrounds. The author also gives anecdotes and tests that involve and teach.

GENDER ISSUES AND DIFFERENCES

Astrachan, A. (1988). *How men feel.* Garden City, NY: Anchor Press/Doubleday.

How men feel about women is the topic of this book, which contains a number of chapters focusing on work relationships.

Farrell, W. (1986). *Why men are the way they are.* New York: McGraw-Hill.

This book offers insights and understanding, not only about male behavior, but also about male-female relationships.

Gilligan, C. (1962). *In a different voice: Psychological theory and women's development.* Cambridge, MA: Harvard University Press.

This book presents a seminal discussion of gender differences in moral/ethical development and the implications for the workplace.

Gray, J. (1992). *Men are from Mars, women are from Venus: A practical guide for improving communication and getting what you want in your relationships.* New York: HarperCollins.

This look at male-female differences argues that communication problems between the sexes are rooted in gender-related value differences.

Gutek, B. A. (1985). *Sex and the workplace.* San Francisco, CA: Jossey-Bass.
This book examines a critical aspect of male-female interaction on the job—the impact of sexual behavior and harassment on women, men, and organizations. The issue is looked at from managerial, legal, psychological, and social perspectives.

Heim, P., & Galant, S. (1992). *Hardball for women: Winning at the game of business.* Los Angeles, CA: Lowell House.
Differences between male and female leadership skills are the subject of this book. Tracing gender differences to the play of boys and girls, the authors apply these preferences to adult behaviors in the workplace.

Landrine, H., & Klonoff, E. A. (1997). *Discrimination against women: Prevalence, consequences and remedies.* Thousand Oaks, CA: Sage.
The authors offer an empirically validated scale for measuring the health effects of sexism and report their findings on the mental and physical health impact of discrimination.

Lipman-Blumen, J. (1984). *Gender roles and power.* Englewood Cliffs, NJ: Prentice Hall.
This book explains the way in which the gender system is a foundation for all other power relationships.

Loden, M. (1985). *Feminine leadership: Or how to succeed in business without being one of the boys.* New York: Times Books.
This book delineates differences between male and female leadership styles and makes suggestions for enhancing the workplace.

Milwid, B. (1990). *Working with men: Professional women talk about power, sexuality, and ethics.* Hillsboro, OR: Beyond Words.
Interviews with 125 professional women provide a look at what it is like for women in the workplace. This book gives an insider's look at the pressures, problems, and hopes of women in the work world.

Morrison, A. M., White, R. P., & van Velson, E. (1987). *Breaking the glass ceiling.* Reading, MA: Addison-Wesley.
Based on a study of executives, this book examines the factors that determine the success and failure of women in corporate America.

Pearson, J. C. (1985). *Gender and communication.* Dubuque, IA: William C. Brown.

This book focuses on the gender gap in interactions, discussing the difficulties and differences in communication between men and women.

Powell, G. (1988). *Women and men in management: The dynamics of interaction.* Thousand Oaks, CA: Sage.

In this book, the author downplays the importance of male-female differences.

Rosener, J. B. (1995). *America's competitive secret: Utilizing women as a management strategy.* New York: Oxford University Press.

This book describes the unique contribution of female professionals and explains why men and women are perceived and evaluated differently at work. It helps both men and women understand the economic, social, and psychological impact of women and men as peers and competitors. It includes chapters on sexual static and how men and women feel.

Sargent, A. G. (1977). *Beyond sex roles.* St. Paul, MN: West.

Through exercises and narrative explanations, the author and other contributors teach, raise awareness, and prod self-exploration about sex roles and change regarding those roles.

Simons, G. F., & Weissman, G. D. (1990). *Men and women: Partners at work.* Los Altos, CA: Crisp.

The objective of this book is to help men and women approach one another openly, creatively, and with effective communication tools. Exercises and worksheets help readers identify and resolve gender issues that inhibit productivity and understanding.

Tannen, D. (1991). *You just don't understand: Women and men in conversation.* New York: William Morrow.

In a down-to-earth, reader-friendly style, the author explains gender differences in communication that produce obstacles. Recognizing and understanding these differences can be a help in avoiding barriers to clear communication between men and women.

Tingley, J. (1994). *Genderflex: Men and women speaking each other's language at work.* New York: AMACOM.

This book gives suggestions about overcoming the gender gap in work communication.

GENERAL BOOKS ABOUT DIVERSITY

Allport, G. W. (1998). *The nature of prejudice.* Reading, MA: Addison-Wesley.

This classic study of the roots of discrimination, originally published in 1954, offers important information, understanding, and insights about dealing with prejudice and stereotyping.

Arredondo, P. (1996). *Successful diversity management initiatives: A blueprint for planning and implementation.* Thousand Oaks, CA: Sage.

This recent addition to the field presents specific steps to plan, direct, and guide organizations through diversity implementation, giving vignettes based on organizational experiences.

Baytos, L. M. (1995). *Designing and implementing successful diversity programs.* Englewood Cliffs, NJ: Prentice Hall.

This thorough how-to manual provides practical guidance and tools to assist practitioners charged with implementing diversity. Organizational examples are provided, as well as checklists and assessments.

Brown, C. D., Snedeker, C. C., & Sykes, B. D. (1997). *Conflict and diversity.* Cresskill, NJ: Hampton Press.

This book presents chapters, each by outstanding communication and diversity management experts, that address different facets of workplace conflicts. It offers theoretical approaches, research, and case studies to help the reader understand diversity-related barriers, as well as tools to deal with them.

Gardenswartz, L., & Rowe, A. (1998). *Managing diversity: A complete desk reference and planning guide* (rev. ed.). New York: McGraw-Hill.

This comprehensive guide, which includes both conceptual information and practical techniques, gives myriad strategies and activities for managing diversity. Over eighty worksheets, checklists, and charts are provided for use by managers, trainers, consultants, and HR professionals.

Gudykunst, W. B. (1991). *Bridging differences: Effective intergroup communication.* Thousand Oaks, CA: Sage.

The author explains the process underlying communication between people of different groups and presents principles for building community with people from diverse backgrounds.

Gudykunst, W. B., Stewart, L. P., & Ting-Toomey, S. (Eds.). (1985). *Communication, culture, and organizational processes.* Thousand Oaks, CA: Sage.

This collection of articles weaves theoretical issues with practical, organizational concerns, such as conflict, negotiation, and decision making in multicultural settings.

Hall, E. T. (1969). *The hidden dimension.* Garden City, NY: Anchor Press/Doubleday.
This book explains proxemics, the ways humans use space in public and private. It provides insights about how this aspect of culture affects personal and business relationships and cross-cultural interactions as well as architecture and urban planning.

Hall, E. T. (1973). *The silent language.* Garden City, NY: Anchor Press/Doubleday.
Information about the cultural aspects of communication is put forth in this fundamental work. The author explains how dimensions such as time and space communicate beyond words.

Hall, E. T. (1989). *Beyond culture.* Garden City, NY: Anchor Press/Doubleday.
This foundation piece on cross-cultural communication analyzes in depth the culturally determined yet unconscious attitudes that mold our thoughts, feelings, communication, and behavior. It continues along with Hall's other two books, *The Silent Language* and *The Hidden Dimension,* to discuss the covert cultural influences that affect cross-cultural encounters.

Harris, P. R., & Moran, R. T. (1987). *Managing cultural differences: High-performance strategies for today's global manager.* Houston, TX: Gulf.
This business-oriented text on diversity gives a comprehensive treatment of cultural differences affecting business, focusing more on international than domestic intercultural issues. It includes questionnaires, surveys, and resources.

Hayles, R., & Russell, A. M. (1997). *The diversity directive: Why some initiatives fail and what to do about it.* Burr Ridge, IL: Irwin Professional.
Drawing on extensive corporate experience, the authors outline the steps necessary for implementing effective diversity initiatives.

Herbert, P. H. (1997). *The color of words: An encyclopedic dictionary of ethnic bias in the United States.* Yarmouth, ME: Intercultural Press.
This thought-provoking book explains the power of language and how it is used to express bias and hatred toward "others." Over 850 words, expressions, and phrases that carry bias are explained.

Hofstede, G. (1984). *Culture's consequences: International differences in work-related values.* Thousand Oaks, CA: Sage.
A foundation piece in the literature about culture, this research-based book discusses culturally based differences in values that affect the workplace. Aspects such as individualism, power distance, masculinity, and avoidance of uncertainty are examined.

Hofstede, G. (1991). *Cultures and organizations: Software of the mind.* New York: McGraw-Hill.
In this work the author shows that effective intercultural cooperation is possible and explains under what circumstances and at what cost it can be achieved.

Hubbard, E. E. (1997). *Measuring diversity results.* Petaluma, CA: Global Insights Publishing.
This book provides practical guidance in measurement, a key aspect of diversity implementation.

Jamieson, D., & O'Mara, J. (1991). *Managing workforce 2000: Gaining the diversity advantage.* San Francisco: Jossey-Bass.
This pioneering book outlines a method for managing diversity using the authors' flex management approach. A number of organizational examples demonstrating effective practices are provided.

Knowles, L., & Prewitt, K. (1969). *Institutional racism in America.* Englewood Cliffs, NJ: Prentice Hall.
This book gives a comprehensive account of the pervasiveness of racism in institutions in this society.

Loden, M., & Rosener, J. B. (1991). *Workforce America! Managing employee diversity as a vital resource.* Burr Ridge, IL: Irwin Professional.
This foundation piece in the literature about diversity makes a case for creating an organization that capitalizes on the richness in differences. It offers an insightful look at the issues that emerge, as well as managerial and organizational strategies to deal with them.

Pedersen, P. (1988). *A handbook for developing multicultural awareness.* Alexandria, VA: American Association for Counseling and Development.
This book, written for counselors, also serves as a resource for managers working with staff from other cultures as well as for employees working with multicultural co-workers and customers.

Ponterotto, J. G., & Pedersen, P. B. (1993). *Preventing prejudice: A guide for counselors and educators.* Thousand Oaks, CA: Sage.

This relevant and pragmatic book serves as an excellent resource for understanding the nature of prejudice and provides developmentally sequenced exercises for dealing with problems of prejudice.

Prasad, P., Mills, A. J., Elmes, M. B., & Prasad, A. (Eds.). (1997). *Managing the organizational melting pot: Dilemmas of workplace diversity.* Thousand Oaks, CA: Sage.
This collection of writings provides an array of theoretical frameworks for illuminating the difficulties of workplace diversity.

Samovar, L. A., & Porter, R. E. (1976). *Intercultural communication: A reader.* Belmont, CA: Wadsworth.
This anthology brings together a series of forty-four articles on culture in general, as well as on specific cultures and aspects of intercultural communication. Both theoretical and practical information are included.

Thiederman, S. (1990). *Bridging cultural barriers for corporate success: How to manage the multicultural work force.* Lexington, MA: Lexington.
This handbook for cross-cultural communication gives practical information about motivating, attracting, interviewing, retaining, and training a multicultural workforce. This reader-friendly book is full of applicable examples, how-to's, and exercises for overcoming obstacles to intercultural communication.

Thomas, R. R. (1991). *Beyond race and gender: Unleashing the power of your total work force by managing diversity.* New York: AMACOM.
This book puts forth a fundamental plan for managing diversity, coupled with practical examples of how organizations capitalize on their diverse staffs. It includes a strategy for a cultural audit as well as an action plan for change.

Ting-Toomey, S., & Korzenny, F. (Eds.). (1991). *Cross-cultural interpersonal communication.* Thousand Oaks, CA: Sage.
This collection of articles covers current research and theories in cross-cultural communication.

Turkewych, C., & Guerrero-Klinoroski, H. (1992). *Intercultural interviewing: The key to effective hiring in a multicultural workforce.* Halle, Quebec, Canada: International Briefing Associates.
With guidelines and critical incidents, this manual serves as a task-specific resource for managers, human resource personnel, and trainees regarding each stage of the interviewing process.

HEALTH CARE ISSUES IN DIVERSITY

Decalmer, P., & Glendinning, F. (Eds.). (1993). *The mistreatment of elderly people.* Thousand Oaks, CA: Sage.

This book discusses elder abuse, including the clinical and legal implications, as well as the issues for nurses and physicians.

Galanti, G. (1991). *Caring for patients from different cultures: Case studies from American hospitals.* Philadelphia, PA: University of Pennsylvania Press.

This pertinent book, written by a professor of nursing and anthropology, describes over 135 actual cultural conflicts that occurred in American hospitals. Its purpose is to help health care professionals understand the cultural dimensions of problems that occur between staff and patients and their families. It also contains an extensive bibliography for those desiring more specific information.

Gropper, R. C. (1996). *Culture and the clinical encounter: An intercultural sensitizer for the health professions.* Yarmouth, ME: Intercultural Press.

Through the use of critical incidents, the author, a medical anthropologist, gives western-trained health care providers insightful examples of health care beliefs and practices of many cultures. Each incident presents a cross-cultural problem in a clinical context for which the reader must choose the best of four possible explanations. The choices are then explained, with reasons given for why a choice is the best course of action or not.

Helman, C. G. (1994). *Culture, health and illness.* Oxford, England: Butterworth-Heinemann.

This medical anthropological work provides in-depth exploration of the ways in which different cultural, social, and ethnic groups explain the cause of illness, the kind of treatment believed in, and the healers they prefer. Chapters include topics such as "Gender and Reproduction," "Doctor-Patient Interaction," and "Cultural Definitions of Anatomy and Physiology."

Kao, H.S.R., & Sinka, S. E. (Eds.). (1996). *Asian perspectives on psychology.* Thousand Oaks, CA: Sage.

This collection of articles by experts from different Asian countries presents perspectives on socialization, development, emotion, personality, and approaches to health.

Kaslow, D. R., & Salett, E. P. (Eds.). (1989). *Crossing cultures in mental health.* Washington, DC: Sietar International.

Through a series of articles, this book offers insight and suggestions for improving cross-cultural communication, especially with regard to immigrant and refugee populations. Both general and culture-specific information is given.

Lorber, J. (1997). *Gender and the social construction of illness.* Thousand Oaks, CA: Sage.

In this book, the author brings a feminist perspective in examining the interface between gender and Western medicine. Chapters include "The Doctor Knows Best: Gender and the Medical Encounter," and "If a Situation Is Defined as Real: Premenstrual Syndrome and Menopause."

National Coalition of Hispanic Health and Human Services Organizations. (1990). *Delivering preventive health care to Hispanics: A manual for providers.* Washington, DC: Author.

This rich resource in notebook form contains critical information about providing health care to Hispanics. Chapters include information on beliefs and practices, strategies for effective patient provider interaction, community education, and specific health problems.

Salimbene, S., & Graczykowski, J. W. (1998). *What language does your patient hurt in?: A health practitioner's guide to treating patients from other cultures.* Amherst, MA: Amherst Educational Publishing.

This user-friendly guide addresses the practical issues involved in the interaction between culture and health care. Both fundamental information about general cultural influences on medical care and specific information about the major culture/language groups in the United States are provided.

Secundy, M. G., & Nixon, L. L. (1992). *Trials, tribulations and celebrations: African-American perspectives on health, illness, aging and loss.* Yarmouth, ME: Intercultural Press.

This collection of short stories, narratives, and poems explores aspects of the life cycle from an African-American perspective. It is especially helpful for health care providers providing services in a multicultural society.

Waxler-Morrison, N., Anderson, J., & Richardson, E. (Eds.). (1990). *Cross-cultural caring: A handbook for health professionals.* Vancouver, British Columbia: UBC Press.

This handbook provides information on recent immigrant groups in Western Canada, such as Vietnamese, Chinese, Japanese,

West Indians, and Iranians. Each chapter, written by a health care professional from that culture, focuses on the health care beliefs and practices as well as the social context of each group.

Wiseman, R. L. (Ed.). (1995). *Intercultural communication theory.* Thousand Oaks, CA: Sage.

This series of scholarly papers on intercultural communication includes a pertinent chapter on cultural differences impacting health communication, giving culture-specific examples.

LATINO ISSUES

Condon, J. C. (1985). *Good neighbors: Communication with the Mexicans.* Yarmouth, MA: Intercultural Press.

In this concise book, the author describes how the cultures of the United States and Mexico differ, how Mexicans and U. S. citizens misunderstand one another, and what can be done to bridge the gap. Vital information for those working with Mexicans is provided in a readable, interesting way.

Knouse, S. B., Rosenfeld, P., & Culbertson, A. (Eds.). (1992). *Hispanics in the workplace.* Thousand Oaks, CA: Sage.

A comprehensive exploration of Hispanic employment factors, problems at work, support systems, and Hispanic women and work. Contributors deal with specific topics, such as recruiting, training, and language barriers.

Kras, E. S. (1989). *Management in two cultures: Bridging the gap between U.S. and Mexican managers.* Yarmouth, ME: Intercultural Press.

This book pinpoints the principal differences between Mexican and U.S. cultures and management styles that cause misunderstandings and conflict. It gives concrete recommendations to both U.S. and Mexican managers for dealing more effectively with one another.

Miranda, A. (1985). *The Chicano experience: An alternative perspective.* Notre Dame, IN: University of Notre Dame Press.

The social and economic conditions facing Mexican-Americans are explained in this book.

Sharris, E. (1992). *Latinos: A biography of the people.* New York: W.W. Norton.

This book offers a deeper understanding of many Spanish-speaking cultures. The origin of the main groups, their history, and their situations now are told mainly through biographies of individuals and families.

OTHER DIVERSE GROUPS

Althen, G. (1988). *American ways: A guide for foreigners in the United States.* Yarmouth, ME: Intercultural Press.
This book is designed for those wanting to understand the behaviors and values of Americans. In easy-to-understand language and clear examples, the author describes the basic characteristics of U.S. culture and offers suggestions for effective interactions with Americans.

Andres, T. (1981). *Understanding Filipino values: A management approach.* Quezon City, Metro Manila, Philippines: New Day.
This book is a resource for understanding Filipino culture and values, with an emphasis on management issues.

Barker, R. G. (1953). *Adjustment to physical handicap and illness: A survey of the social psychology of physique and disability.* New York: Social Science Research Council.
This book combines a theoretical and a practical discussion of the social psychology of differently abled people. It also contains a chapter on employment.

Baylan, E. (1991). *Women and disability.* Atlantic Highlands, NJ: Zed Books.
This book discusses the issues faced by women with disabilities.

Blumfeld, W. J., & Raymond, D. (1988). *Looking at gay and lesbian life.* Boston, MA: Beacon.
Lesbian and gay lifestyles in the United States are examined and discussed.

Condon, J. C. (1984). *With respect to the Japanese: A guide for Americans.* Yarmouth, MA: Intercultural Press.
In this handbook, the author discusses aspects of Japanese values and behavior that affect communication, business relations, and management styles. He goes on to make recommendations on how to deal with the Japanese during face-to-face encounters.

Fieg, J. P., & Mortlock, E. (1989). *A common core: Thais and Americans.* Yarmouth, ME: Intercultural Press.

Both commonalties and differences between Thai and American cultures are explained in this book. The authors discuss the implications of the differences for people engaged in cross-cultural encounters on and off the job.

Fisher, G. (1980). *International negotiations: A cross-cultural perspective.* Yarmouth, ME: Intercultural Press.

By comparing how Japanese, Mexicans, French, and Americans reach agreements, the author demonstrates how culture influences the negotiation process and suggests a useful line of questioning and analysis for intercultural negotiation.

Gochenour, T. (1990). *Considering Filipinos.* Yarmouth, ME: Intercultural Press.

This intercultural handbook contrasts the values and perspectives of Filipinos and Americans and offers guidelines for successful interaction between these two groups. It gives suggestions for bridging cultural differences in social and workplace settings, as well as case studies showing cross-cultural dynamics in action.

Kitano, H. L., & Daniels, R. (1988). *Asian Americans: Emerging minorities.* Englewood Cliffs, NJ: Prentice Hall.

This book focuses on the various Asian ethnic groups, discussing their experiences in the U.S.

Lanier, A. R. (1988). *Living in the USA.* Yarmouth, ME: Intercultural Press. This book is designed to help foreigners and newcomers understand the United States. It provides a guide to customs, courtesies, and caveats and gives practical advice to anyone coming to the United States.

McLuhan, T. C. (1971). *Touch the earth.* New York: Simon & Schuster. This book recollects the Native American way of life and contrasts it with mainstream American society and values.

Mead, M. (1970). *Culture and commitment: A study of the generation gap.* Garden City, NY: Doubleday.

This anthropologist's look at the generation gap explains the differences in views and perspectives between the young and the old.

Nelson, R. (1978). *Creating acceptance for handicapped people.* Springfield, IL: Charles C. Thomas.

This handbook is designed to teach the community to be supportive and accepting of people with disabilities, either physical or mental.

Nydell, M. K. (1987). *Understanding Arabs: A guide for westerners.* Yarmouth, ME: Intercultural Press.
This readable cross-cultural handbook gives a concise and insightful look at Arab culture. It dispels common Western misconceptions regarding Arab behavior and explains the values, beliefs, and practices of Arabs, particularly in terms of their impact on interactions with Europeans and North Americans.

Renwick, G., Pedersen, P., & Smith, K. (1998). *Communicating with Malaysians.* Yarmouth, ME: Intercultural Press.
This addition to the InterActs series offers insights and practical help in interacting with Malaysians.

Richmond, Y. (1992). *From nyet to da: Understanding the Russians.* Yarmouth, ME: Intercultural Press.
This succinctly written book is a cross-cultural guide for dealing with Russians. The author outlines ways of responding most effectively to Russians on a personal level as well as in business.

Richmond, Y. (1995). *From da to yes: Understanding the East Europeans.* Yarmouth, ME: Intercultural Press.
Another in the InterActs series, this book offers help in understanding and dealing with people from Eastern Europe. It contains chapters on Poles, Czechs, Slovaks, Hungarians, Romanians, Moldavians, Bulgarians, Serbs, Croats, Slovenians, Albanians, Ukrainians, and others.

Root, M.P.P. (1997). *Filipino Americans: Transforming identity.* Thousand Oaks, CA: Sage.
This collection of articles from historians, social workers, psychologists, educators, and ethnic scholars addresses issues such as ethnic identity, relationships, and mental health.

Sagarin, E. (Ed.). (1971). *The other minorities.* Waltham, MA: Xerox College.
Nonethnic minorities, such as the differently abled, are the subjects in this collection of articles.

Shahar, L., & Kurz, D. (1995). *Border crossings: American interactions with Israelis.* Yarmouth, ME: Intercultural Press.

In case studies based on real situations, the authors show Americans and Israelis attempting to communicate across cultural barriers. They also offer coping strategies and exercises that help readers choose the most appropriate for their own personal styles.

Stewart, E. C. (1972). *American cultural patterns: A cross-cultural perspective.* Yarmouth, ME: Intercultural Press.

Using the value orientation framework of Kluckholn and Strodtbeck, the author examines American patterns of thinking and behaving. He goes on to analyze the assumptions about human nature and the physical world that underlie these values and to compare and contrast them with those of other cultures.

Ting, Liu Wu, D. (1997). *Asian Pacific Americans in the workplace.* Walnut Creek, CA: Altanura Press.

Through numerous interviews, the author presents stories of racial discrimination, sexual harassment, and familial expectations experienced by Asian-Pacific Americans on the job. Exercises and suggested strategies are also included.

Wenzhong, H., & Grove, C. L. (1991). *Encountering the Chinese: A guide for Americans.* Yarmouth, ME: Intercultural Press.

This useful book goes beyond description to explain Chinese behavior. It provides a cross-cultural analysis that can guide Westerners toward more effective relationships with the Chinese.

Winfeld, L., & Spielman, S. (1995). *Straight talk about gays in the workplace: Creating an inclusive environment for everyone in your organization.* New York: American Management Association.

This candid book brings the myths and facts about gays out into the open and offers a clear look at how companies can include issues of sexual orientation in their non-discrimination and diversity management programs.

TRAINING AND FACILITATION OF DIVERSE GROUPS

Jones, J. E., Bearley, W., & Watsabaugh, D. (1996). *The new fieldbook for trainers.* Amherst, MA: HRD Press.

This resource provides over sixty tools, activities, and designs as well as content information about involving participants, processing learning, and facilitating meetings.

Justice, T., & Jamieson, D. (1998). *The complete guide to facilitation.* Amherst, MA: HRD Press.

This comprehensive resource helps facilitators manage their groups' processes and includes a section on handling conflicts and other common problems with groups.

Pike, B., & Arch, D. (1997). *Dealing with difficult participants.* San Francisco: Jossey-Bass/Pfeiffer.

This book offers over 120 practical strategies for minimizing resistance and maximizing the learning potential and results of presentations.

Chapter 13
Other Diversity Resources

THIS CHAPTER PROVIDES AN ARRAY OF ADDITIONAL RESOURCES that may be helpful as training vehicles and sources of information. They are grouped by type in the following listings:

- Assessment Tools and Instruments
- Periodicals, Journals, and Newsletters
- Structured Experiences and Games
- Videos and Films
- Websites and Other Resources

ASSESSMENT TOOLS AND INSTRUMENTS

The Cross-Cultural Adaptability Inventory. Colleen Kelley and Judith Meyers, 2500 Torrey Pines Road, La Jolla, CA 92037. (619) 453-8165.
This self-response questionnaire measures fifteen attitudes and attributes important to cross-cultural adjustment. Resulting in a profile of cross-cultural adaptability, this standardized and normed instrument can be applied in selection, placement, counseling, workforce planning, career development, and self-selection.

Cultural Context Work Style Inventory. Claire B. Halverson. School for International Training, Experiment in International Living, Brattleboro, VT. (802) 254-6098.
This self-scored, twenty-item questionnaire is designed for self-understanding based on the high–low context framework of Edward Hall. It includes background information, charts, and a bibliography.

Diversity Awareness Profile and *Diversity Awareness Profile, Manager's Version.* Karen Grote. Jossey-Bass/Pfeiffer, 350 Sansome Street, San Francisco, CA 94104. (800) 274-4434.

A forty-item questionnaire places respondents in one of five categories on the "Diversity Awareness Spectrum." The profile suggests action steps and includes notes for trainers.

Overseas Assignment Inventory (OAI). Moran, Stahl & Boyer, International Division, 900 28th Street, Boulder, CO 80303. (303) 449-8440.

This self-scoring instrument is for people planning to work and live abroad. It measures four critical dimensions of cross-cultural adaptability. A manual is included.

The Questions of Diversity: Assessment Tools for Organizations and Individuals. George Simons, ODT Incorporated, P.O. Box 134, Amherst, MA 01004. (413) 549-1293.

This resource contains nine surveys that assess personal and organizational issues of diversity in the workplace. These instruments are intended as learning tools.

PERIODICALS, JOURNALS, AND NEWSLETTERS

The COSSMHO Reporter. The National Coalition of Hispanic Health and Human Service Organizations, 1501 Sixteenth Street NW, Washington, DC 20036. (202) 389-5000.

This biannual newsletter provides information about issues concerning health care for Hispanics.

Cross-Cultural Research: The Journal of Comparative Social Science. Sage Publications, Inc., P.O. Box 5084, Thousand Oaks, CA 91359. (805) 499-9774.

This scholarly journal publishes refereed studies pertaining to cross-cultural issues in the social and behavioral sciences.

Cultural Diversity at Work. The GilDeane Group, 13751 Lake City Way NE, Suite 106, Seattle, WA 98125-8612. (206) 362-0336.

This bimonthly newsletter offers articles and resource reviews on relevant and topical issues facing today's diverse organizations. Its practical focus aims at preparing the reader for "managing, training, and conducting business in the global age." Subscription also includes eleven monthly issues of *The Diversity Networker,* which lists upcoming diversity conferences, seminars, and events.

Culturally Competent Care. Inter-Face International, 3821 East State Street, Suite 197, Rockford, IL 61108. (815) 965-7535.

This bimonthly newsletter provides concrete, culture-specific information to help providers reach out to patients from other cultures. While intended for those in health care, its information can be of value to customer service staff and managers in other settings as well.

The Diversity Marketing Outlook. The GilDeane Group, 13751 Lake City Way NE, Suite 106, Seattle, WA 98125-8612. (206) 362-0336.

This quarterly magazine focuses on advertising and marketing to today's increasingly diverse consumer base. It features examples of creative approaches and new developments in the arena of multicultural marketing.

Journal of Cross-Cultural Psychology. Sage Publications, Inc., P.O. Box 5084, Thousand Oaks, CA 91359. (805) 499-9774.

This journal presents behavioral and social research focusing on psychological phenomena as differentially influenced by culture.

Managing Diversity. Jamestown Area Labor Management Committee, Inc., P.O. Box 819, Jamestown, NY 14702-0819. (716) 665-3654.

This monthly newsletter directed at business leaders and managers offers a series of articles on pertinent issues faced in leading and managing diverse organizations. Through thoughtful articles and practical approaches, it challenges and educates the reader.

STRUCTURED EXPERIENCES AND GAMES

Bafa Bafa: Cross-Cultural Orientation. Gary R. Shirts, P.O. Box 910, Del Mar, CA 92014. (619) 755-0272.

This experiential activity simulates the contact between two very different cultures, Alpha and Beta. The activity is structured so that participants learn through direct simulated experience and then apply that learning to real-life situations. (*Rafa Rafa*, a simplified version for children in grades 5 through 8, is also available.)

Barnga: A Simulation Game on Cultural Clashes. Sivasailam Thiagarajan, Intercultural Press, P.O. Box 700, Yarmouth, ME 04096. (207) 846-5168. Through playing a simple card game in small groups, participants experience the effect of simulated cultural differences on human interactions. This activity is easy to run in a relatively short time.

Diversity Bingo. Jossey-Bass/Pfeiffer, 350 Sansome Street, San Francisco, CA 94104. (800) 274-4434.

This fast-paced, interactive group experience helps individuals recognize the complexities involved in determining cultural perceptions and assumptions.

The Diversity Game. Quality Educational Development, 41 Central Park West, New York, NY 10023. (212) 724-3335.

This multiplayer board game provides insights, raises awareness, and stimulates discussion about diversity issues in the workplace. Questions focus on real workplace issues, such as communication, motivation, reward, recognition, respect, and trust in the context of gender, race, and cultural diversity.

Diversophy. Multus, Inc., 46 Treetop Lane, Suite 200, San Mateo, CA 94402-3234. (415) 342-2040.

This board game is designed to be played by line managers, supervisors, administrative personnel, salespeople, customer service representatives, and senior executives. Easy to play, the game delivers thought-provoking information, deals with critical attitudes, and teaches useful skills for meeting the challenges of diversity.

Ecotonos. Dianne Hofner-Saphiere and Nipporica Associates. Intercultural Press, P.O. Box 700, Yarmouth, ME. (207) 846-5168.

This simulation deals with problem solving and decision making in multicultural groups.

The Global Diversity Game. Quality Educational Development, 41 Central Park West, New York, NY 10023. (212) 724-3335.

In this board game, teams answer questions focusing on demographics, jobs, legislation, and society as they relate to the global business environment. Cross-cultural and transnational information is highlighted, stimulating a dynamic exchange of knowledge and experience among participants.

Health Care Diversity. Suzanne Salimbene and George Simons. Maltus, Inc., and George Simons International, 46 Treetop Lane, Suite 200, San Mateo, CA 94402. (415) 342-2040.

This interactive board game helps participants learn cultural specifics about diversity in health care in an involving, stimulating way.

Redundancia. Deanne Hofner-Saphiere and Nipporica Associates, 10072 Buena Vista Drive, Conifer, CO 80433. (303) 838-1798.

This short, effective simulation helps people understand the challenges faced by individuals attempting to communicate in a second language.

VIDEOS AND FILMS

Bill Cosby on Prejudice. Budget Films, 4590 Santa Monica Boulevard, Los Angeles, CA 90029. (213) 660-0187.

This film presents a monologue on prejudice by Bill Cosby.

Bridges: Skills for Managing a Diverse Workforce. BNA Communications, 9439 Key West Avenue, Rockville, MD 20850. (800) 253-6067.

This eight-module video-based program is designed to train managers and supervisors in managing diverse workers. It raises awareness about cultural/racial/gender differences and presents the skills to deal with them. The series includes manuals for trainees and participants.

Bridging Cultural Barriers: Managing Ethnic Diversity in the Workplace. Barr Films, 12801 Schabarum Avenue, P.O. Box 7878, Irwindale, CA 91706-7878. (800) 234-7878.

This half-hour film featuring Sondra Thiederman, Ph.D., teaches about the effective management of diverse workers through simulated examples of a manager resolving situations with two culturally different staff members. Vignettes are interspersed with brief lectures by Dr. Thiederman.

The Cost of Intolerance. BNA Communications, 9439 Key West Avenue, Rockville, MD 20850-3396. (800) 233-6067.

This six-unit video program helps employees improve customer service and increase sales by valuing diverse customers. Issues such as handling customers who speak with thick accents and overcoming subtle biases and stereotypes are dealt with through realistic vignettes.

Cultural Diversity in the Hospital Setting: Fostering Understanding and Developing Cross-Cultural Management Skills. Sondra Thiederman, Ph.D., distributed by Hospital Educational Services, P.O. Box 396, La Jolla, CA 92038.

This two-hour video of an actual workshop with employees of Green Hospital, Scripps Clinic, La Jolla, California, focuses on intercultural communication. Many examples and practical suggestions are given.

Dealing with Diversity. American Media Incorporated, 4900 University Avenue, West Des Moines, IA 50266-6769. (800) 262-2557.

This video training program helps employees deal with diversity by understanding how others want to be treated. It focuses on understanding and respecting individual differences and improving communication by asking questions and listening.

Diverse Teams at Work. corVision, 1339 Barclay Boulevard, Buffalo Grove, IL 60089. (800) 537-3130.

This video, based on the book of the same title, demonstrates the impact of the many dimensions of diversity on the interactions of a work team. Understanding these differences is developed as a critical step toward building respect between people of different backgrounds.

Faces. Salenger Films, 1635 12th Street, Santa Monica, CA 90404. (310) 450-1300.

This one-minute, unnarrated video shows a kaleidoscope of human faces of different sexes, races, and ages merging and complementing one another to form an integrative whole. By showing the individual worth of each face, as well as its contribution to the total picture, the video demonstrates that we are all unique, yet we share a common bond.

Getting Along: Words of Encouragement. Cross Cultural Communications, 4585 48th Street, San Diego, CA 92114. (800) 858-4478.

In four and a half minutes of printed messages and music, this video reminds people to work and live together with open hearts and open minds.

Let's Talk Diversity. American Media Incorporated, 4900 University Avenue, West Des Moines, IA 50266-6769. (800) 262-2557.

This video training program helps all employees understand how values, attitudes, and behaviors affect others. It also helps them recognize biases and stereotypes based on gender, race, religion, age, culture, disability, and lifestyle.

Living and Working in America. Via Press, 400 E. Evergreen Boulevard, Suite 314, Vancouver, WA 98660. (800) 944-8421.

A comprehensive three-volume audiovisual series for training nonnative speakers of English in communication skills needed for supervisory/management positions in the multicultural workforce. Includes video scenes, textbook, audiotapes, and an instructor's manual with experiential learning activities.

Managing Diversity. CRM Films, 2233 Faraday Avenue, Carlsbad, CA 92008. (800) 421-0833.

This film combines dramatizations of information from experts in the field to focus on diversity issues, such as stereotyping and communication, as well as differences in perceptions regarding teamwork, power, and authority. It ends with a useful list of things people can do to improve communication in a diverse environment. A guide is included.

Managing a Multicultural Workforce: The Mosaic Workplace. Films for the Humanities and Sciences, P.O. Box 2053, Princeton, NJ 08543-2053. (800) 257-5126.

This training program of ten videos addresses the issues of the diverse workplace. It covers topics such as understanding different cultural values and styles, men and women working together, and success strategies for minorities.

The Multicultural Customer. Salenger Films, 1635 12th Street, Santa Monica, CA 90404. (310) 450-1300.

This video helps customer service staff understand the dynamics of cross-cultural communication and get beyond barriers to establishing positive relationships with diverse customers. It shows vignettes of typical customer/staff interactions and gives tips for providing top-notch service to a diverse population.

Sandcastle: A Film about Teamwork and Diversity. Salinger Films, 1635 12th Street, Santa Monica, CA 90404. (310) 450-1300.

Teamwork and the contribution of each diverse team member are illustrated in this Academy Award-winning, unnarrated thirteen-minute video. A unique story about the building of a sand castle, the film demonstrates the value of diversity.

Serving Customers with Disabilities. Salenger Films, 1635 12th Street, Santa Monica, CA 90404. (310) 450-1300.

The film offers etiquette and customer service skills to help employees serve customers with disabilities more effectively.

A Tale of "O." Goodmeasure, Inc., P.O. Box 3004, Cambridge, MA 02139.

This film/video deals with differentness by showing how a few O's learn to function in organizations made up of X's.

True Colors. Coronet/MTI Film and Video, 420 Academy Drive, Northbrook, IL 60062. (800) 777-2400.

In this provocative edition of ABC's "Prime Time," host Diane Sawyer follows two college-educated men in their mid-thirties, one black, one white, as they involve themselves in a variety of everyday situations to test levels of prejudice based on skin color. The results are startling and unsettling.

Valuing Diversity. Copeland Griggs Productions, 302 23rd Avenue, San Francisco, CA 94121. (415) 668-4200.
This seven-part film/video series for managers and other employees focuses on the advantages inherent in diversity. Segments deal with issues such as managing/supervising differences, upward mobility in a multicultural organization, and communicating across cultures. The series includes users' guides.

West Meets East in Japan. Pyramid Film and Video, Box 1048, Santa Monica, CA 90406. (800) 421-2304.
This culture-specific video lets you experience Japanese culture from the point of view of an outsider learning the norms of Japanese etiquette. A study guide is included.

Why Do We Kick a Brother or a Sister When They're Down? The Riverbend Press, P.O. Box 586, Concord, MA 01742. (508) 371-2664.
This powerful videotape is the true story of childhood friends and the destructive influences of classism and other prejudices. This training tool about human relations is especially useful in dealing with valuing differences.

A Winning Balance. BNA Communications, 9439 Key West Avenue, Rockville, MD 20850. (800) 233-6067.
This thirty-four–minute, video-based training program introduces the topic of diversity and its importance to all employees. It goes on to deal with attitudes toward differences, the impact of biases, becoming a diversity change agent, and making a personal commitment. Trainer and participant manuals are included.

Working Together: Managing Cultural Diversity. Crisp Publications, 1200 Hamilton Court, Menlo Park, CA 94025. (800) 442-7477.
This video-book program teaches how to work productively in a multicultural environment. Users learn how to manage their attitudes and communication in interactions with people from other cultures. The kit includes a leader's guide.

WEBSITES AND OTHER RESOURCES

Cultural Diversity Hotwire. *http://www.diversityhotwire.com.*
This website of the *Cultural Diversity at Work* newsletter provides an article of the month, abstracts of newsletter articles, and a catalogue of books, videos, and back issues, as well as a networking/ learning events calendar.

Inter-Face International. *http://www.cmihub.com/t/InterFaceInt.htm.*
This website offers a listing of diversity products and services for the health care field.

Multicultural Calendar. Creative Cultural Communications, 12300 Contra Costa Boulevard, Suite 270, Pleasant Hill, CA 94523. (800) 883-4072.
This wall calendar with twelve original ethnic works of art lists holidays and cultural events of a wide variety of religions and cultures.

Multicultural Resource Calendar. Amherst Educational Publishing, 30 Blue Hills Road, Amherst, MA 01002. (800) 865-5549.
This award-winning calendar educates staff by increasing awareness about the contributions of people of over thirty-five different backgrounds and holidays of over thirty-five groups.

National Multicultural Institute. *http:www.nmci.org/nmci/links.htm.*
This site provides many multicultural web links.

The 1998 Health Practitioner's Multi-Cultural Resource Calendar. Suzanne Salimbene, Amherst Educational Publishing, 30 Blue Hills Road, Amherst, MA 01002. (800) 865-5548.
This calendar presents monthly health care tips and provides a separate resource section on health care characteristics of Hispanic, Asian, African American, and Native American patients.

Tools on Disk

SYSTEM REQUIREMENTS. The minimum configuration needed to utilize the files included on this disk is a computer system with one 3.5" floppy disk drive capable of reading double-sided high-density IBM formatted floppy disks and word processing or desktop publishing software able to read Microsoft WORD 6.0/95 files. Document memory needs will vary, but your system should be capable of opening files sizes of 50+K. No monitor requirements other than the ones established by your document software need be met.

PLATFORM. Each of the figures in your manual that are marked with a disk icon have been saved onto the enclosed disk as a Microsoft WORD 6.0/95 file. These files can be opened with many Windows- and Macintosh-based word processors or desktop publishers for viewing or editing as you see fit. Not all software will read the files exactly the same way, but the DOC format is an honest attempt by Jossey-Bass Publishers to preserve document features such as fonts, character attributes, bullets, and so on, as accurately as possible.

INSTRUCTIONS. Copy all DOC files to a directory/folder in your computer system. To read the files using your Windows-based document software, select FILE from the main menu followed by OPEN to display the dialog box. Set the correct drive letter and subdirectory shown in the OPEN dialog box by using the LOOK IN box. In the FILES OF TYPE box enter *.doc to display the list of DOC files available in the subdirectory.

FILE NAMING. Each file name is coded to the page in the *Manual* on which the document appears. For example, "Giving Directions and Explanations in Culturally Sensitive Ways" has been named p108.doc. You can open the file by either double-clicking your mouse on the file name that you want to open or by clicking once on the file name to select it and then clicking on the OPEN command button.